The Che Guevara Myth
and the Future of Liberty

D0710875

The Che Guevara Myth and the Future of Liberty

Alvaro Vargas Llosa

The INDEPENDENT INSTITUTE

Oakland, California

Copyright © 2006 The Independent Institute
All rights reserved. No part of this book may be reproduced or transmitted
in any form by electronic or mechanical means now known or to be invented,
including photocopying, recording, or information storage and retrieval
systems, without permission in writing from the publisher, except by a reviewer
who may quote brief passages in a review. Nothing herein should be construed
as necessarily reflecting the views of the Institute or as an attempt to aid or
hinder the passage of any bill before Congress.

The Independent Institute
100 Swan Way, Oakland, CA 94621-1428
Telephone: 510-632-1366 · Fax: 510-568-6040
Email: info@independent.org
Website: www.independent.org

Library of Congress Cataloging-in-Publication Data

Vargas Llosa, Alvaro.
    The Che Guevara myth and the future of liberty / by Alvaro Vargas Llosa.
        p.   cm.
Includes bibliographical references and index.

ISBN-13: 978-1-59813-005-8 (pbk. : alk. paper)
ISBN-10: 1-59813-005-6 (pbk. : alk. paper)

1. Guevara, Ernesto, 1928–1967. 2. Myth–Political aspects. 3. Latin America—
Economic conditions. 4. Political culture–Latin America. 5. Liberalism–Latin
America–History. I. Title.
F2849.22.G85V37   2005
980.03'5092–dc22

                                                    2005027718

10 9 8 7 6 5 4 3   06 07 08 09 10

 **The INDEPENDENT INSTITUTE**

THE INDEPENDENT INSTITUTE is a non-profit, non-partisan, scholarly research and educational organization that sponsors comprehensive studies of the political economy of critical social and economic issues.

The politicization of decision-making in society has too often confined public debate to the narrow reconsideration of existing policies. Given the prevailing influence of partisan interests, little social innovation has occurred. In order to understand both the nature of and possible solutions to major public issues, The Independent Institute's program adheres to the highest standards of independent inquiry and is pursued regardless of political or social biases and conventions. The resulting studies are widely distributed as books and other publications, and are publicly debated through numerous conference and media programs. Through this uncommon independence, depth, and clarity, The Independent Institute expands the frontiers of our knowledge, redefines the debate over public issues, and fosters new and effective directions for government reform.

FOUNDER & PRESIDENT
David J. Theroux

RESEARCH DIRECTOR
Alexander Tabarrok

SENIOR FELLOWS
Bruce L. Benson
Ivan Eland
Robert Higgs
Alvaro Vargas Llosa
Richard K. Vedder

ACADEMIC ADVISORS

Herman Belz
UNIVERSITY OF MARYLAND

Thomas E. Borcherding
CLAREMONT GRADUATE
SCHOOL

Boudewijn Bouckaert
UNIVERSITY OF GHENT,
BELGIUM

James M. Buchanan
GEORGE MASON UNIVERSITY

Allan C. Carlson
HOWARD CENTER

Robert D. Cooter
UNIVERSITY OF CALIFORNIA,
BERKELEY

Robert W. Crandall
BROOKINGS INSTITUTION

Richard A. Epstein
UNIVERSITY OF CHICAGO

B. Delworth Gardner
BRIGHAM YOUNG
UNIVERSITY

George Gilder
DISCOVERY INSTITUTE

Nathan Glazer
HARVARD UNIVERSITY

Ronald Hamowy
UNIVERSITY OF ALBERTA,
CANADA

Steve H. Hanke
JOHNS HOPKINS UNIVERSITY

Ronald Max Hartwell
OXFORD UNIVERSITY

James J. Heckman
UNIVERSITY OF CHICAGO

H. Robert Heller
INTERNATIONAL PAYMENTS
INSTITUTE

Lawrence A. Kudlow
KUDLOW & COMPANY

Deirdre N. McCloskey
UNIVERSITY OF ILLINOIS,
CHICAGO

J. Huston McCulloch
OHIO STATE UNIVERSITY

Forrest McDonald
UNIVERSITY OF ALABAMA

Thomas Gale Moore
HOOVER INSTITUTION

Charles Murray
AMERICAN ENTERPRISE
INSTITUTE

Michael J. Novak, Jr.
AMERICAN ENTERPRISE
INSTITUTE

June E. O'Neill
BARUCH COLLEGE

Charles E. Phelps
UNIVERSITY OF ROCHESTER

Paul Craig Roberts
INSTITUTE FOR POLITICAL ECONOMY

Nathan Rosenberg
STANFORD UNIVERSITY

Simon Rottenberg
UNIVERSITY OF
MASSACHUSETTS

Paul H. Rubin
EMORY UNIVERSITY

Bruce M. Russett
YALE UNIVERSITY

Pascal Salin
UNIVERSITY OF PARIS,
FRANCE

Arthur Seldon
INSTITUTE OF ECONOMIC
AFFAIRS, ENGLAND

William F. Shughart II
UNIVERSITY OF MISSISSIPPI

Joel H. Spring
STATE UNIVERSITY OF NEW
YORK, OLD WESTBURY

Vernon L. Smith
GEORGE MASON UNIVERSITY

Richard L. Stroup
MONTANA STATE UNIVERSITY

Thomas S. Szasz
STATE UNIVERSITY OF N.Y.,
SYRACUSE

Robert D. Tollison
UNIVERSITY OF CLEMSON

Arnold S. Trebach
AMERICAN UNIVERSITY

Gordon Tullock
GEORGE MASON UNIVERSITY

Richard E. Wagner
GEORGE MASON UNIVERSITY

Sir Alan A. Walters
AIG TRADING CORPORATION

Walter E. Williams
GEORGE MASON UNIVERSITY

Charles Wolf
RAND CORPORATION

THE INDEPENDENT INSTITUTE
100 Swan Way, Oakland, California 94621-1428, U.S.A.
Telephone: 510-632-1366 • Facsimile: 510-568-6040
Email: info@independent.org • Website: www.independent.org

Contents

1 Introduction   1

2 The Killing Machine: Che Guevara, from
   Communist Firebrand to Capitalist Brand   7

3 Latin American Liberalism—A Mirage?   23

4 The Individualist Legacy in Latin America   53

   Index   71

   About the Author   79

1

Introduction

When I was 14, I had a group of friends with colorful international backgrounds at my boarding school. We were rebellious and shared a strong mistrust of authority in its various forms. We resented the stringent rules, the collectivist atmosphere, the sense of regimentation. It was open war between us and the schoolmasters. They called us MCG (Mature Cosmopolitan Group) with a touch of sarcasm. We idolized Bob Marley, occasionally experimented with ganja, recited Keats' "Ode on a Grecian Urn" to ourselves ("Thou still unravish'd bride of quietness..."), and regularly sneaked off the school grounds at night looking for adventure and getting a fair share of it, not always sweet. We would go back to school in the wee hours of the morning, just in time to get caught by whichever housemaster happened to be looking for us or reporting us to the police as missing!

One of the kids in the group was from South America and he had two passions in life. One was Clint Eastwood, who was alive and kicking. The other was Che Guevara, who had died long before. Like the Clint Eastwood of the movies, my friend lived on the edge. Like Che Guevara (and Keats), he would meet his death prematurely, tragically. He was the only one in a group made up of Europeans, Asians, Africans, and Latin Americans who would wrap himself in Che Guevara paraphernalia. For some reason I was not quite able to articulate, I never wore the Guevara beret, smoked the cigar, or hung the poster on my wall.

A few years later, I spent a semester studying at an American university. Che Guevara made a new attempt to seduce me. This time, my friends were mostly politically active Puerto Ricans who wanted their island to be independent. One of them hung a poster of Che Guevara on his wall and, next to it, a picture of "Comrade Gonzalo," the genocidal leader of Shining Path, Peru's Maoist organization. As I came into the room one afternoon and this couple faced me from the wall, I was paralyzed. It suddenly dawned on me why my South American friend from boarding school had never quite been able to persuade me to take up Che.

There it was, pure and simple: just like Abimael Guzmán, Che was the negation of what I most seemed to long for in this complicated world—freedom and peace. I must have vaguely sensed this at school, but now, for the first time, I was able to fully grasp a precious truth: one should never be confused by the many variations of that species, the tyrant. Stalinist Che Guevara and Maoist Abimael Guzmán belonged to different camps and represented contrasting attitudes to life—the former being the quintessential pinup, the latter a bizarre recluse—but what they had in common, their lust for totalitarian power, was much more important than their differences.

I had experienced firsthand Shining Path's campaign of terror against the very poor peasants in whose name it purported to act. Like millions of Peruvians, I had personally been affected in different ways by this unlikely reincarnation of Cambodia's Pol Pot in the middle of the Andes. Seeing Che Guevara next to Guzmán on a chic campus wall brought to light the ugly truth about the Argentine hero of the Cuban Revolution, but, more importantly, it inspired the poignant realization that all those prepared to use force to take life and property away from their fellow men are soul mates whatever the ideological or moral subterfuge used to conceal their real motives. "Really, you should rip that off. You have no idea," I said to my friend, and I left the room quite disturbed.

Many years later, when I had had the chance to encounter numerous other disguises for tyranny, some on the left but others on the right, I focused on that image from university as the starting point of a larger reflection. The conclusion I reached continues to haunt me today: there are myriad forms of oppression, some much more subtle than others, sometimes adorned with the theme of social justice and at other times obscured by the language of security, and recognizing and denouncing the deceitful psychological mechanisms with which the enemies of liberty attempt to bamboozle us into voluntary servitude is one of the urgent tasks of our times.

Discerning the truth from among the more or less sophisticated impostures that speak to the liberation of humanity from despotism, injustice, hunger, is the first step towards a free society. The liberation of the individual is first and foremost a liberation of the mind, as Etienne de la Boétie taught us centuries ago in his masterful *The Politics of Obedience: The Discourse of Voluntary Servitude*. Only then can one resort to fruitful action in the field of social betterment.

One major reason why at least half of mankind lives in poverty and billions live under tyranny is that many impostures continue to deceive so many people. Those who represent them have been able to fool many credulous souls into thinking their liberation will come from the use of violence, the exercise of state dominance, vertical authority, or, more subtly, grand schemes of wealth redistribution—i.e. the "political" rather than the "economic" means, in Franz Oppenheimer's famous and still relevant distinction between a predatory system that exploits a productive class in order to sustain a parasitical oligarchy and a productive system that guarantees the rights of life, freedom, and property, therefore making justice possible.

One of the ironies of choosing to distinguish between freedom and oppression rather than between Socialist and conservative, left and right, pious or impious, is that one stumbles upon the fact that Che Guevara had a lot more in common with the men and systems he fought than would seem conceivable. He was in essence no different from the Batista dictatorship he combated as a young guerrilla in the Cuban jungle—except that he was more efficient and ideological about being a callous dictator himself.

That is, indeed, the tragic history of Latin America: an endless sequence of oppressive states, each one purporting to suppress the evils of preceding institutions. The Iberian colonial system preserved the worst features of the pre-Columbian world. The republics in turn perpetuated the colonial legacy they were meant to abolish. Centralization, verticality, patronage, and monopolies have survived in varying degrees the ideological and political changes that have taken place over time, even under democratic regimes.

The essays that follow seek to convey the idea that intellectual and political deceit—the bondage of the mind—represent the first step towards oppression—the bondage of the body—and that the way to begin to restore a measure of rationality and common sense to those countries where oppression still prevails is to expose the lies on which it rests. It occurred to me that trying to expose the truth about Che Guevara to many young people would be as good a way as any to get this message across.

In 1813, Thomas Jefferson wrote to the Marquis de Lafayette: "Their people are immersed in the darkest ignorance and brutalized by bigotry and superstition." He was referring to Latin America, where just half a century earlier the Spanish and Portuguese colonies seemed a world ahead of the English colonies of North America. Latin America's superiority had been, of course, an illusion—the illusion that a highly centralized, hierarchical society where a person's life was determined by the authorities had something to do with civilization. The splendor of those baroque edifices that looked like a metaphor of cultural greatness had deluded most intellectuals and leaders in Iberian America.

Today, when half of Latin America still lives in poverty and when a significant portion of the other half makes ends meet but still lacks the kinds of opportunities available elsewhere, many people nonetheless look up to the state as the agent of social justice. While Che

Guevara appears to have become benign capitalist merchandise for many young people in rich countries, he is still a flesh and blood being, incarnated in the prevailing institutions, for millions of Latin Americans and citizens of other unfortunate territories.

This short book does not want to simply expose an ugly truth. It also looks at the alternative path for the peoples of the underdeveloped world. That is the purpose of "Latin American Liberalism—A Mirage?" and of "The Individualist Legacy of Latin America," the two essays on liberty that follow the text on Che Guevara. The first of these focuses on the reforms that have failed to change things in the underdeveloped world, while the second tries to rescue from oblivion a long tradition of liberty among Latin Americans—an anti-Che tradition, if you will—in the hope that it can serve as an inspiration for a future free society. Exposing the myth is the first step.

The next step is to convey to those who are still under the myth's spell that there is indeed a way to liberate people from injustice and hunger, but that it implies a massive move away from statism and collectivism, and towards decentralized, individual-based rights.

2

The Killing Machine
Che Guevara, from Communist Firebrand to
Capitalist Brand

Che Guevara, who did so much (or was it so little?) to destroy capitalism, is now a quintessential capitalist brand. His likeness adorns mugs, hoodies, lighters, key chains, wallets, baseball caps, toques, bandannas, tank tops, club shirts, couture bags, denim jeans, herbal tea, and of course those omnipresent T-shirts with the photograph, taken by Alberto Korda, of the socialist heartthrob in his beret during the early years of the revolution, as Che happened to walk into the photographer's viewfinder—and into the image that, thirty-eight years after his death, is still the logo of revolutionary (or is it capitalist?) chic. Sean O'Hagan claimed in *The Observer* that there is even a soap powder with the slogan "Che washes whiter."

Che products are marketed by big corporations and small businesses, such as the Burlington Coat Factory, which put out a television commercial depicting a youth in fatigue pants wearing a Che T-shirt, or Flamingo's Boutique in Union City, New Jersey, whose owner responded to the fury of local Cuban exiles with this devastating argument: "I sell whatever people want to buy." Revolutionaries join the merchandising frenzy, too—from "The Che Store," catering to "all your revolutionary needs" on the Internet, to the Italian writer Gianni Minà, who sold Robert Redford the movie rights to Che's diary of his juvenile trip around South America in 1952 in exchange for access to the shooting of the film *The Motorcycle Diaries* so that Minà could produce his own documentary. Not to mention Alberto

Granado, who accompanied Che on his youthful trip and advises documentarists, and who now complains in Madrid, according to *El País*, over Rioja wine and duck magret, that the American embargo against Cuba makes it hard for him to collect royalties. To take the irony further: the building where Guevara was born in Rosario, Argentina, a splendid early twentieth-century edifice at the corner of Urquiza and Entre Ríos Streets, was until recently occupied by the private pension fund AFJP Máxima, a child of Argentina's privatization of social security in the 1990s.

The metamorphosis of Che Guevara into a capitalist brand is not new, but the brand has been enjoying a revival of late—an especially remarkable revival, since it comes years after the political and ideological collapse of all that Guevara represented. This windfall is owed substantially to *The Motorcycle Diaries*, the film produced by Robert Redford and directed by Walter Salles. (It is one of three major motion pictures on Che either made or in the process of being made in the last two years; the other two have been directed by Josh Evans and Steven Soderbergh.) Beautifully shot against landscapes that have clearly eluded the eroding effects of polluting capitalism, the film shows the young man on a voyage of self-discovery as his budding social conscience encounters social and economic exploitation—laying the ground for a New Wave re-invention of the man whom Sartre once called the most complete human being of our era.

But to be more precise, the current Che revival started in 1997, on the thirtieth anniversary of his death, when five biographies hit the bookstores, and his remains were discovered near an airstrip at Bolivia's Vallegrande airport, after a retired Bolivian general, in a spectacularly timed revelation, disclosed the exact location. The anniversary refocused attention on Freddy Alborta's famous photograph of Che's corpse laid out on a table, foreshortened and dead and romantic, looking like Christ in a Mantegna painting.

It is customary for followers of a cult not to know the real life story of their hero, the historical truth. (Many Rastafarians would renounce Haile Selassie if they had any notion of who he really was.) It is not surprising that Guevara's contemporary followers, his new post-communist admirers, also delude themselves by clinging to a myth—except the young Argentines who have come up with an expression that rhymes perfectly in Spanish: *"Tengo una remera del Che y no sé por qué,"* or "I have a Che T-shirt and I don't know why."

Consider some of the people who have recently brandished or invoked Guevara's likeness as a beacon of justice and rebellion against the abuse of power. In Lebanon, demonstrators protesting against Syria at the grave of former prime minister Rafiq Hariri carried Che's image. Thierry Henry, a French soccer player who plays for Arsenal, in England, showed up at a major gala organized by FIFA, the world's soccer body, wearing a red and black Che T-shirt. In a recent review in *The New York Times* of *George A. Romero's Land of the Dead*, Manohla Dargis noted that "the greatest shock here may be the transformation of a black zombie into a righteous revolutionary leader," and added, "I guess Che really does live, after all." The soccer hero Maradona showed off the emblematic Che tattoo on his right arm during a trip where he met Hugo Chávez in Venezuela. In Stavropol, in southern Russia, protesters denouncing cash payments of welfare concessions took to the central square with Che flags. In San Francisco, City Lights Books, the legendary home of beat literature, treats visitors to a section devoted to Latin America in which half the shelves are taken up by Che books. José Luis Montoya, a Mexican police officer who battles drug crime in Mexicali, wears a Che sweatband because it makes him feel stronger. At the Dheisheh refugee camp on the West Bank, Che posters adorn a wall that pays tribute to the Intifada. A Sunday magazine devoted to social life in Sydney, Australia, lists the three dream guests at a dinner party: Alvar Aalto, Richard Branson, and Che Guevara. Leung Kwok-hung, the rebel elected to Hong Kong's Legislative Council, defies Beijing by wearing a Che T-shirt. In Brazil, Frei Betto, President Lula da Silva's adviser in charge of the high-profile "Zero Hunger" program, says that "we should have paid less attention to Trotsky and much more to Che Guevara." And most famously, at this year's Academy Awards ceremony Carlos Santana and Antonio Banderas performed the theme song from *The Motorcycle Diaries*, and Santana showed up wearing a Che T-shirt and a crucifix. The manifestations of the new cult of Che are everywhere. Once again the myth is firing up people whose causes for the most part represent the exact opposite of what Guevara was.

No man is without some redeeming qualities. In the case of Che Guevara, those qualities may help us to measure the gulf that separates reality from myth. His honesty (well, partial honesty) meant that he left written testimony of his cruelties, including the really ugly, though not the ugliest, stuff. His courage—what Castro described as "his way, in every difficult and dangerous moment, of doing the most difficult and dangerous thing"—meant that he did not live to take full responsibility for Cuba's hell. Myth can tell you as much about an era as truth. And so it is that thanks to Che's own testimonials to his thoughts and his deeds, and thanks also to his premature departure, we may know exactly how deluded so many of our contemporaries are about so much.

Guevara might have been enamored of his own death, but he was much more enamored of other people's deaths. In April 1967, speaking from experience, he summed up his homicidal idea of justice in his "Message to the Tricontinental": "hatred as an element of struggle; unbending hatred for the enemy, which pushes a human being beyond his natural limitations, making him into an effective, violent, selective, and cold-blooded killing machine." His earlier writings are also peppered with this rhetorical and ideological violence. Although his former girlfriend Chichina Ferreyra doubts that the original version of the diaries of his motorcycle trip contains the observation that "I feel my nostrils dilate savoring the acrid smell of gunpowder and blood of the enemy," Guevara did share with Granado at that very young age this exclamation: "Revolution without firing a shot?

You're crazy." At other times the young bohemian seemed unable to distinguish between the levity of death as a spectacle and the tragedy of a revolution's victims. In a letter to his mother in 1954, written in Guatemala, where he witnessed the overthrow of the revolutionary government of Jacobo Arbenz, he wrote: "It was all a lot of fun, what with the bombs, speeches, and other distractions to break the monotony I was living in."

Guevara's disposition when he traveled with Castro from Mexico to Cuba aboard the Granma is captured in a phrase in a letter to his wife that he penned on January 28, 1957, not long after disembarking, which was published in her book *Ernesto: A Memoir of Che Guevara in Sierra Maestra*: "Here in the Cuban jungle, alive and bloodthirsty." This mentality had been reinforced by his conviction that Arbenz had lost power because he had failed to execute his potential enemies. An earlier letter to his former girlfriend Tita Infante had observed that "if there had been some executions, the government would have maintained the capacity to return the blows." It is hardly a surprise that during the armed struggle against Batista, and then after the triumphant entry into Havana, Guevara murdered or oversaw the executions in summary trials of scores of people—proven enemies, suspected enemies, and those who happened to be in the wrong place at the wrong time.

In January 1957, as his diary from the Sierra Maestra indicates, Guevara shot Eutimio Guerra because he suspected him of passing on information: "I ended the problem with a .32 caliber pistol, in the right side of his brain.... His belongings were now mine." Later he shot Aristidio, a peasant who expressed the desire to leave whenever the rebels moved on. While he wondered whether this particular victim "was really guilty enough to deserve death," he had no qualms about ordering the death of Echevarría, a brother of one of his comrades, because of unspecified crimes: "He had to pay the price." At other times he would simulate executions without carrying them out, as a method of psychological torture.

Luis Guardia and Pedro Corzo, two researchers in Florida who are working on a documentary about Guevara, have obtained the testimony of Jaime Costa Vázquez, a former commander in the revolutionary army known as "El Catalán," who maintains that many of the executions attributed to Ramiro Valdés, a future interior minister of Cuba, were Guevara's direct responsibility, because Valdés was under his orders in the mountains. "If in doubt, kill him" were Che's instructions. On the eve of victory, according to Costa, Che ordered the execution of a couple dozen people in Santa Clara, in central Cuba, where his column had gone as part of a final assault on the island. Some of them were shot in a hotel, as Marcelo Fernándes-Zayas, another former revolutionary who later became a journalist, has written—adding that among those executed, known as *casquitos*, were peasants who had joined the army simply to escape unemployment.

But the "cold-blooded killing machine" did not show the full extent of his rigor until, immediately after the collapse of the Batista regime, Castro put him in charge of La Cabaña prison. (Castro had a clinically good eye for picking the right person to guard the revolution against infection.) San Carlos de La Cabaña was a stone fortress used to defend Havana against English pirates in the eighteenth century; later it became a military barracks. In a manner chillingly reminiscent of Lavrenti Beria, Guevara presided during the first half of 1959 over one of the darkest periods of the revolution. José Vilasuso, a lawyer and a professor at Universidad Interamericana de Bayamón in Puerto Rico, who belonged to the body in charge of the summary judicial process at La Cabaña, told me recently that

> Che was in charge of the Comisión Depuradora. The process followed the law of the Sierra: there was a military court and Che's guidelines to us were that we should act with conviction, meaning that they were all murderers and the revolutionary way to proceed was to be implacable. My direct supe-

rior was Miguel Duque Estrada. My duty was to legalize the files before they were sent on to the Ministry. Executions took place from Monday to Friday, in the middle of the night, just after the sentence was given and automatically confirmed by the appellate body. On the most gruesome night I remember, seven men were executed.

Javier Arzuaga, the Basque chaplain who gave comfort to those sentenced to die and personally witnessed dozens of executions, spoke to me recently from his home in Puerto Rico. A former Catholic priest, now seventy-five, who describes himself as "closer to Leonardo Boff and Liberation Theology than to the former Cardinal Ratzinger," he recalls that

there were about eight hundred prisoners in a space fit for no more than three hundred: former Batista military and police personnel, some journalists, a few businessmen and merchants. The revolutionary tribunal was made of militiamen. Che Guevara presided over the appellate court. He never overturned a sentence. I would visit those on death row at the *galera de la muerte*. A rumor went around that I hypnotized prisoners because many remained calm, so Che ordered that I be present at the executions. After I left in May, they executed many more, but I personally witnessed fifty-five executions. There was an American, Herman Marks, apparently a former convict. We called him "the butcher" because he enjoyed giving the order to shoot. I pleaded many times with Che on behalf of prisoners. I remember especially the case of Ariel Lima, a young boy. Che did not budge. Nor did Fidel, whom I visited. I became so traumatized that at the end of May 1959 I was ordered to leave the parish of Casa Blanca, where La Cabaña was located and where I had held Mass for three years. I went to Mexico for treatment. The day I left, Che told me we had both tried to bring one another to each other's side and had failed. His last words were: "When we take our masks off, we will be enemies."

How many people were killed at La Cabaña? Pedro Corzo offers a figure of some two hundred, similar to that given by Armando Lago, a retired economics professor who has compiled a list of 217 names as part of an eight-year study on executions in Cuba. Vilasuso told me that four hundred people were executed between January and the end of June in 1959 (at which point Che ceased to be in charge of La Cabaña). Secret cables sent by the American Embassy in Havana to the State Department in Washington spoke of "over 500." According to Jorge Castañeda, one of Guevara's biographers, a Basque Catholic sympathetic to the revolution, the late Father Iñaki de Aspiazú, spoke of seven hundred victims. Félix Rodríguez, a CIA agent who was part of the team in charge of the hunt for Guevara in Bolivia, told me that he confronted Che after his capture about "the two thousand or so" executions for which he was responsible during his lifetime. "He said they were all CIA agents and did not address the figure," Rodríguez recalls. The higher figures may include executions that took place in the months after Che ceased to be in charge of the prison.

Which brings us back to Carlos Santana and his chic Che gear. In an open letter published in *El Nuevo Herald* on March 31 of this year, the great jazz musician Paquito D'Rivera castigated Santana for his costume at the Oscars, and added: "One of those Cubans [at La Cabaña] was my cousin Bebo, who was imprisoned there precisely for being a Christian. He recounts to me with infinite bitterness how he could hear from his cell in the early hours of dawn the executions, without trial or process of law, of the many who died shouting, 'Long live Christ the King!'"

Che's lust for power had other ways of expressing itself besides murder. The contradiction between his passion for travel—a protest of sorts against the constraints of the nation-state—and his impulse to become himself an enslaving state over others is poignant. In writing about Pedro de Valdivia, the conquistador of Chile, Guevara reflected: "He belonged to that special class of men the species produces every so often, in whom a craving for limitless power is so extreme that any suffering to achieve it seems natural." He might have been describing himself. At every stage of his adult life, his megalomania manifested itself in the predatory urge to take over other people's lives and property, and to abolish their free will.

In 1958, after taking the city of Sancti Spiritus, Guevara unsuccessfully tried to impose a kind of *sharia*, regulating relations between men and women, the use of alcohol, and informal gambling—a puritanism that did not exactly characterize his own way of life. He also ordered his men to rob banks, a decision that he justified in a letter to Enrique Oltuski, a subordinate, in November of that year: "The struggling masses agree to robbing banks because none of them has a penny in them." This idea of revolution as a license to re-allocate property as he saw fit led the Marxist Puritan to take over the mansion of an emigrant after the triumph of the revolution.

The urge to dispossess others of their property and to claim ownership of others' territory was central to Guevara's politics of raw power. In his memoirs, the Egyptian leader Gamal Abdel Nasser records that Guevara asked him how many people had left his country because of land reform. When Nasser replied that no one had left, Che countered in anger that the way to measure the depth of change is by the number of people "who feel there is no place for them in the new society." This predatory instinct reached a pinnacle in 1965, when he started talking, God-like, about the "New Man" that he and his revolution would create.

Che's obsession with collectivist control led him to collaborate on the formation of the security apparatus that was set up to subjugate six and a half million Cubans. In early 1959, a series of secret meetings took place in Tarará, near Havana, at the mansion to which Che temporarily withdrew to recover from an illness. That is where the top leaders, including Castro, designed the Cuban police state. Ramiro Valdés, Che's subordinate during the guerrilla war, was put in charge of G-2, a body modeled on the Cheka. Francisco Ciutat, a veteran of the Spanish Civil War sent by the Soviets and who had been very close to Ramón Mercader, Trotsky's assassin, and later befriended Che, played a key role in organizing the system, together with Luis Alberto Lavandeira, who had served the boss at La Cabaña. Guevara himself took charge of G-6, the body tasked with the ideological indoctrination of the armed forces. The U.S.-backed Bay of Pigs invasion in April 1961 became the perfect occasion to consolidate the new police state with the rounding up of tens of thousands of Cubans and ordering a new series of executions. As Guevara himself told the Soviet ambassador Sergei Kudriavtsev, counterrevolutionaries were never "to raise their head again."

"Counterrevolutionary" is the term that was applied to anyone who departed from dogma. It was the communist synonym for "heretic." Concentration camps were one form in which dogmatic power was employed to suppress dissent. History attributes to the Spanish general Valeriano Weyler, the captain-general of Cuba at the end of the nineteenth century, the first use of the word "concentration" to describe the policy of surrounding masses of potential opponents—in his case, supporters of the Cuban independence movement—with barbed wire and fences. How fitting that Cuba's revolutionaries more than half a century later were to take up this indigenous tradition. In the beginning, the revolution mobilized volunteers to build schools and to work in ports, plantations, and factories—all exquisite photo-ops for Che the stevedore, Che the cane-cutter, Che the clothmaker. It was not long before volunteer work became a little less voluntary: the first forced labor camp, Guanahacabibes, was set up in western Cuba at the end of 1960. This is how Che explained the function performed by this method of confinement: "[We] only send to Guana-hacabibes those doubtful cases where we are not sure people should go to jail ..., people who have committed crimes against revolutionary morals, to a lesser or greater degree.... It is hard labor, not brute labor, rather the working conditions there are hard."

This camp was the precursor to the eventual systematic confinement, starting in 1965 in the province of Camagüey, of dissidents, homosexuals, AIDS victims, Catholics, Jehovah's Witnesses, Afro-Cuban priests, and other such scum, under the banner of Unidades Militares de Ayuda a la Producción, or Military Units to Help Production. Herded into buses and trucks, the "unfit" would be transported at gunpoint into concentration camps organized on the Guanahacabibes mold. Some would never return; others would be raped, beaten, or mutilated; and most would be traumatized for life, as Néstor Almendros's wrenching documentary *Improper Conduct* showed the world in 1984.

So *Time* magazine may have been less than accurate in August 1960 when it described the revolution's division of labor with a cover story featuring Che Guevara as the "brain" and Fidel Castro as the "heart" and Raúl Castro as the "fist." But the perception reflected Guevara's crucial role in turning Cuba into a bastion of totalitarianism. Che was a somewhat unlikely candidate for ideological purity, given his bohemian spirit, but during the years of training in Mexico and in the ensuing period of armed struggle in Cuba he emerged as the communist ideologue infatuated with the Soviet Union, much to the discomfort of Castro and others who were essentially opportunists using whatever means were necessary to gain power. When the would-be revolutionaries were arrested in Mexico in 1956, Guevara was the only one who admitted that he was a communist and was studying Russian. (He spoke openly about his relationship with Nikolai Leonov from the Soviet Embassy.) During the armed struggle in Cuba, he forged a strong alliance with the Popular Socialist Party (the island's Communist Party) and with Carlos Rafael Rodríguez, a key player in the conversion of Castro's regime to communism.

This fanatical disposition made Che into a linchpin of the "Sovietization" of the revolution that had repeatedly boasted about its independent character. Very soon after the *barbudos* came to power, Guevara took part in negotiations with Anastas Mikoyan, the Soviet deputy prime minister, who visited Cuba. He was entrusted with the mission of furthering Soviet-Cuban negotiations during a visit to Moscow in late 1960. (It was part of a long trip in which Kim Il Sung's North Korea was the country that impressed him "the most.") Guevara's second trip to Russia, in August 1962, was even more significant, because it sealed the deal to turn Cuba into a Soviet nuclear beachhead. He met Khrushchev in Yalta to finalize details on an operation that had already begun and involved the introduction of forty-two Soviet missiles, half of which were armed with nuclear warheads, as well as launchers and some forty-two thousand soldiers. After pressing his Soviet allies on the danger that the United States might find out what was happening, Guevara obtained assurances that the Soviet navy would intervene—in other words, that Moscow was ready to go to war.

According to Philippe Gavi's biography of Guevara, the revolutionary had bragged that "this country is willing to risk everything in an atomic war of unimaginable destructiveness to defend a principle." Just after the Cuban missile crisis ended—with Khrushchev reneging on the promise made in Yalta and negotiating a deal with the United States behind Castro's back that included the removal of American missiles from Turkey—Guevara told a British communist daily: "If the rockets had remained, we would have used them all and directed them against the very heart of the United States, including New York, in our defense against aggression." And a couple of years later, at the United Nations, he was true to form: "As Marxists we have maintained that peaceful coexistence among nations does not include coexistence between exploiters and the exploited."

Guevara distanced himself from the Soviet Union in the last years of his life. He did so for the wrong reasons, blaming Moscow for being too soft ideologically and diplomatically, for making too many concessions—unlike Maoist China, which he came to see as a haven of orthodoxy. In October 1964, a memo written by Oleg Daroussenkov, a Soviet official close to him, quotes Guevara as saying: "We asked the Czechoslovaks for arms; they turned us down. Then we asked the Chinese; they said yes in a few days, and did not even charge us, stating that one does not sell arms to a friend." In fact, Guevara resented the fact that Moscow was asking other members of the communist bloc, including Cuba, for something in return for its colossal aid and political support. His final attack on Moscow came in Algiers, in February 1965, at an international conference, where he accused the Soviets of adopting the "law of value," that is, capitalism. His break with the Soviets, in sum, was not a cry for independence. It was an Enver Hoxha–like howl for the total subordination of reality to blind ideological orthodoxy.

The great revolutionary had a chance to put into practice his economic vision—his idea of social justice—as head of the National Bank of Cuba and of the Department of Industry of the National Institute of Agrarian Reform at the end of 1959, and, starting in early 1961, as minister of industry. The period in which Guevara was in charge of most of the Cuban economy saw the near-collapse of sugar production, the failure of industrialization, and the introduction of rationing—all this in what had been one of Latin America's four most economically successful countries since before the Batista dictatorship.

His stint as head of the National Bank, during which he printed bills signed "Che," has been summarized by his deputy, Ernesto Betancourt: "[He] was ignorant of the most elementary economic principles." Guevara's powers of perception regarding the world economy were famously expressed in 1961, at a hemispheric conference in Uruguay, where he predicted a 10 percent rate of growth for Cuba "without the slightest fear," and, by 1980, a per capita income greater than that of "the U.S. today." In fact, by 1997, the thirtieth anniversary of his death, Cubans were dieting on a ration of five pounds of rice and one pound of beans per month; four ounces of meat twice a year; four ounces of soybean paste per week; and four eggs per month.

Land reform took land away from the rich, but gave it to the bureaucrats, not to the peasants. (The decree was written in Che's house.) In the name of diversification, the cultivated area was reduced and manpower distracted toward other activities. The result was that between 1961 and 1963, the harvest was down by half, to a mere 3.8 million metric tons. Was this sacrifice justified by progress in Cuban industrialization? Unfortunately, Cuba had no raw materials for heavy industry, and, as a consequence of the revolutionary redistribution, it had no hard currency with which to buy them—or even basic goods. By 1961, Guevara was having to give embarrassing explanations to the workers at the office: "Our technical comrades at the companies have made a toothpaste … which is as good as the previous one; it cleans just the same, though after a while it turns to stone." By 1963, all hopes of industrializing Cuba were abandoned, and the revolution accepted its role as a colonial provider of sugar to the Soviet bloc in exchange for oil to cover its needs and to re-sell to other countries. For the next three decades, Cuba would survive on a Soviet subsidy of somewhere between $65 billion and $100 billion.

Having failed as a hero of social justice, does Guevara deserve a place in the history books as a genius of guerrilla warfare? His greatest military achievement in the fight against Batista—taking the city of Santa Clara after ambushing a train with heavy reinforcements—is seriously disputed. Numerous testimonies indicate that the commander of the train surrendered in advance, perhaps after taking bribes. (Gutiérrez Menoyo, who led a different guerrilla group in that area, is among those who have decried Cuba's official account of Guevara's victory.) Immediately after the triumph of the revolution, Guevara organized guerrilla armies in Nicaragua, the Dominican Republic, Panama, and Haiti—all of which were crushed. In 1964, he sent the Argentine revolutionary Jorge Ricardo Masetti to his death by persuading him to mount an attack on his native country from Bolivia, just after representative democracy had been restored to Argentina.

Particularly disastrous was the Congo expedition in 1965. Guevara sided with two rebels—Pierre Mulele in the west and Laurent Kabila in the east—against the ugly Congolese government, which was sustained by the United States as well as by South African and exiled Cuban mercenaries. Mulele had taken over Stanleyville earlier before being driven back. During his reign of terror, as V.S. Naipaul has written, he murdered all the people who could read and all those who wore a tie. As for Guevara's other ally, Laurent Kabila, he was merely lazy and corrupt at the time; but the world would find out in the 1990s that he, too, was a killing machine. In any event, Guevara spent most of 1965 helping the rebels in the east before fleeing the country ignominiously. Soon afterward, Mobutu came to power and installed a decades-long tyranny. (In Latin American countries too, from Argentina to Peru, Che-inspired revolutions had the practical result of reinforcing brutal militarism for many years.)

In Bolivia, Che was defeated again, and for the last time. He misread the local situation. There had been an agrarian reform years before; the government had respected many of the peasant communities' institutions; and the army was close to the United States despite its nationalism. "The peasant masses don't help us at all" was Guevara's melancholy conclusion in his Bolivian diary. Even worse, Mario Monje, the local communist leader, who had no stomach for guerrilla warfare after having been humiliated at the elections, led Guevara to a vulnerable location in the southeast of the country. The circumstances of Che's capture at Yuro ravine, soon after meeting the French intellectual Régis Debray and the Argentine painter Ciro Bustos, both of whom were arrested as they left the camp, was, like most of the Bolivian expedition, an amateur's affair.

Guevara was certainly bold and courageous, and quick at organizing life on a military basis in the territories under his control, but he was no General Giap. His book *Guerrilla Warfare* teaches that popular forces can beat an army, that it is not necessary to wait for the right conditions because an insurrectional *foco* (or small group of revolutionaries) can bring them about, and that the fight must primarily take place in the countryside. (In his prescription for guerrilla warfare, he also reserves for women the roles of cooks and nurses.) However, Batista's army was not an army, but a corrupt bunch of thugs with no motivation and not much organization; and guerrilla *focos*, with the exception of Nicaragua, all ended up in ashes for the *foquistas*; and Latin America has turned 70 percent urban in these last four decades. In this regard, too, Che Guevara was a callous fool.

In the last few decades of the nineteenth century, Argentina had the second-highest growth rate in the world. By the 1890s, the real income of Argentine workers was greater than that of Swiss, German, and French workers. By 1928, that country had the twelfth-highest per capita GDP in the world. That achievement, which later generations would ruin, was in large measure due to Juan Bautista Alberdi.

Like Guevara, Alberdi liked to travel: he walked through the pampas and deserts from north to south at the age of fourteen, all the way to Buenos Aires. Like Guevara, Alberdi opposed a tyrant, Juan Manuel Rosas. Like Guevara, Alberdi got a chance to influence a revolutionary leader in power—Justo José de Urquiza, who toppled Rosas in 1852. And like Guevara, Alberdi represented the new government on world tours, and died abroad. But unlike the old and new darling of the left, Alberdi never killed a fly. His book, *Bases y puntos de partida para la organización de la República Argentina*, was the foundation of the Constitution of 1853 that limited government, opened trade, encouraged immigration, and secured property rights, thereby inaugurating a seventy-year period of astonishing prosperity. He did not meddle in the affairs of other nations, opposing his country's war against Paraguay. His likeness does not adorn Mike Tyson's abdomen.

3

Latin American Liberalism—
A Mirage?

It is said that Latin America's misfortune is instability. I believe the opposite. "Next to instability," Germán Arciniegas wrote in 1958, "there at times occurs something worse: stability" (all translations from Spanish-language material are mine). A word with a double meaning, *stability* signifies continuity yet also denotes a static or immutable quality. In the two centuries of Latin America's existence as independent republics, a permanent institutional and political order has followed a path of continuity under the constant swings of the present and the mirages of turbulent change. At the same time, we Latin Americans have not known how to be unstable where we should be. For this reason, Latin America's standard of living is one-tenth that of the United States and Canada; one-half of our population is poor, and one-quarter lives in misery (Sol M. Linowitz Forum 1997). A decade after the poorly named "liberal" reforms south of the Rio Grande, dismay is spreading from one end of Latin America to another. The developed countries are stable in essential matters and unstable in the rest—perfectly inverse to our own realities. In the United States at the beginning of the twentieth century, railroad stocks, the symbol of heavy industry, were the only stocks that a conservative investor took into account in the so-called blue chips. At the close of the century, with a recorded increase of 26,130 percent in the Dow Jones index, the stars of the American stock market were companies with no profits, examples being such dissimilar endeavors as Amazon and the Internet Capital Group (Norris 2000). Can there be any greater instability? Yet, thanks to fundamental stability, this transition, a revolution that has changed the symbols of the modern economy, has taken place, transferring the locus of universal progress from industrial goods to the world of the mind and the imagination. In Latin America, however, our sense of what must be changeable and what must be constant in a society has determined that the only progress recorded during the past century was that forced by the progress of the developed countries. Whereas some countries of the world rode on the back of the universal technological Pegasus, we clutched its hooves and were dragged along. Ours was a passive progress.

Auth is the word I would use to describe the basic characteristic of our institutional organization and, by extension, of our societies. Caudillismo, the overwhelming influence of the strongman in government that emerged from our battles for independence, is still the mark of our political life, even in democracy. Together with the strong positivist influence inherited from the nineteenth century, caudillismo has placed the will over legislation and legislation over law to the point that we have been governed by a teleocracy (a government of objectives) instead of by a nomocracy (a government of laws)—to apply the formula used by Bertrand de Jouvenel. Heliocentric like the Inca society, which revolved around a Sun god incarnated by the emperor, our societies have circled the orbit of political and military power. For us, order has not been that "balance generated from inside" a society, but rather the "pressure exerted from outside it," according to Ortega y Gasset's conception ([1927] 1974). Therefore, the distinguishing Latin American figures at the end of the twentieth century were authoritarian caudillos—from Fidel Castro to Augusto Pinochet and from Alberto Fujimori to Hugo Chávez—a strange cocktail of populism, nationalism, theatricality, and antiliberalism arising in the homeland of Francisco de Miranda and Andrés Bello (also the homeland, to be sure, of the military caudillos Simón Bolivar and Antonio José de Sucre).

In our countries' collectivism—or disdain for the individual—
has been another constant, the offspring of an ancient tradition. The
Greeks gave personal, individual characteristics to abstractions of the
mind. At some point, human intelligence began to do the opposite:
to give an abstract, later collective, meaning to the individual and to
the human. Perhaps Roman law, a great achievement in many ways,
later contributed through legal abstractions to the birth of collectivist
concepts such as *race, nation,* and *people.* In any case, the collectivist
rationalism of the eighteenth and nineteenth centuries took deeper
root in us than did ideas of freedom. Since then, collectivism has
been a political seal, a product and extension of our authoritarianism. Is it strange, then, that in this context during the 1990s the rule
of law and the market economy were magically separated? Not at
all. The magic consisted of making it appear that they are different.
When it was no longer possible to deny the failure of collectivism,
we Latin Americans in the 1990s embarked on a supposedly great
reform in the name of a market economy, viewing it separately from
a government of laws, which is in truth the other name for a free
economy. The result has been not just a partial and frustrated reform,
but an ideological confusion whose denouncement and rectification
are perhaps the greatest of all the tasks engaging Latin American liberals today. Many people had a notion of what a market economy is
and how it works, but few understood the transition from a closed to
an open society. Consequently, we have had many surprises during
this transition. It is one thing to design a free society from scratch,
another to journey toward it from a closed society, in the here and
now. This journey is what has failed, not the free society (which we
still do not have).

Nothing provides greater evidence of our disdain for the rule of
law than the continuous changes to our constitutions or, worse, the
perpetuation of ourselves in power or the attempt to create the world
from nothing with each new government, but without truly altering
anything essential, so that our constitutions today are—as they were

in the nineteenth century, after independence—a dead letter at best, mere legal cover-ups for the murder of the individual at worst. "I have been told that you are good at drawing up constitutions," Napoleon said to Father Siéyes. "For the new order I need you to write a short, obscure constitution for me" (qtd. in Fernández 1999). Likewise, our leaders draw up custom-made constitutions. Even worse, they make them not short and obscure but interminable and detailed, like a military plan.

The Weight of Our History

Throughout the 1990s, a more critical view of our political, economic, and cultural tradition advanced, although its practical expression left much to be desired. This is no small matter because the politically authoritarian and economically mercantilist tradition has long standing. Our theocratic pre-Columbian states, despite their differences (the city-states of the Mayan civilization were more scientific, and the Aztec and Inca Empires were better organized socially) were centralist and vertical, collectivist and despotic. Superimposed on this sociopolitical structure were the Spanish colonies, which were (as was the Portuguese colony in Brazil) quite different from the ones established by the Anglo-Saxon settlers in the North American colonies. The peninsular vision that arrived on our coasts was well summarized by Claudio Véliz in defining baroque art, the symbol of Counter-Reformation Spain: "The Baroque is a reminder of imperial greatness, an obstacle to dissolution, a technique for the preservation of unity, an alibi for the central control of diversity, a justification for the pursuit of glory, a noble excuse for the recurrence of defeat. . . . An assertion of stability, a refusal to give way, a glorification of obstinacy, an affirmation of belief, an indictment of change as an illusion. The Baroque is the mode of the hedgehog" (1994). In the North, in contrast, the "Ruskin gothic" vision prevailed, a world of asymmetry, eccentricity, and diversity, common law instead of civil codes, romanticism rather than canonical classicism (Véliz 1994).

Through a monopoly of commodity exchanges, the Spanish Empire controlled the trafficking of goods, capital, and human beings between the mother country and the colonies through the ports of Porto Bello, Panama and Veracruz, Mexico (Pendle 1976). The Crown also controlled religion through the Patronato de Indias (Council of Indias), and the Roman Catholic Church introduced the Inquisition (in cases such as the Jesuit settlements in Paraguay, it established quasi-totalitarian systems). Even language was part of the political power, as demonstrated by Antonio de Nebrija, who upon completing the first grammar of the Castilian language, offered it to the Crown, stating "language is the companion to the empire" (Véliz 1994). The result was smuggling, which in the seventeenth century represented two-thirds of commerce, along with the buying and selling of public offices and the disregard for law and authority. "I obey, but I do not comply," said officials of the colony. The Bourbon reforms of the eighteenth century, which promoted local administration, perhaps helped to accelerate the independence movements carried out by the Creoles, who distrusted the Peninsular authorities, but although some mestizos, such as the Mexican priests Morelos and Hildalgo, were among the rebels, independence was not a movement primarily from the bottom up, but rather a rebellion of one privileged caste against another. One report illustrates the enormous difference between what occurred in 1776 in England's North American colonies and what happened in the Spanish colonies of Latin America in 1820: in the revolutionary North, there were three thousand newspapers; in revolutionary Mexico, there were only three (Harrison 1997).

The colonial experience seems especially futile if we consider the fascinating intellectual phenomenon that had previously taken place in imperial Spain: a group of Scholastics writing about economics had anticipated the Austrian school by almost three centuries. The influence of Christian humanism and the Thomist idea of natural law are also apparent in the thinking of these writers, several of them belonging to the School of Salamanca, to which Jesús Huerta de Soto (1999) has recently directed appreciative attention. Diego de Covarrubias y Leyva formulated the subjectivist theory of value; Luis Saravia de la Calle demolished the medieval superstition of a "just price"; Jerónimo Castillo de Bovadilla praised free competition; Francisco de Vitoria challenged slavery in the name of natural law; and Juan de Mariana defended "tyrannicide" in the name of justice (Huerta de Soto 1999). These scholastics also anticipated the Chicago school in subjects such as inflation.

Despite its great achievements, this tremendously rich tradition of thought from our Mengers and Böhm-Bawerks *avant la lettre* continued to be disregarded. During the nineteenth century, great rational constructions and Comtian positivism bewitched our thinkers' minds and infected our leaders, turning their thinking about the state into a sort of "geometry" (Ortega y Gasset [1927] 1974). I am not speaking of liberal rationality as defended by Ayn Rand (1961) in opposing Kant and his rejection of all possible rationality, certainty, or exact science, but of constructivist rationality of the sort that emerged from the Age of Enlightenment, which is the antithesis of Hume's school of philosophy and which conceived of government as an entity morally responsible for the fate of its subjects through social engineering. Legal and legislative positivism helped to turn our governments into factories for producing rules and laws intended to do good, and our governments steadily reduced the citizens' private room to maneuver. Intellectuals played a preeminent role in this development.

During the nineteenth century, there was no shortage of spokesmen—from Francisco Bilbao in Chile to Faustino Sarmiento and Juan Bautista Alberdi in Argentina—to attack the colonial tradition of the Counter-Reformation, but except in Argentina, thanks to Alberdi's masterpiece *Bases y puntos de partida para la constitución política de la República Argentina* (Bases and Points of Departure for the Political Constitution of the Argentine Republic, [1852] 1996), this thought did not result in practical action. For us, the nineteenth century turned out to be what Francisco de Miranda famously called "chaos, nothing but chaos." Our liberal caudillos, the most famous of which was perhaps Benito Juárez in Mexico, fought ecclesiastical privileges and did much by secularizing our societies, but at the same time they strengthened military authority and oligarchic privileges.

Around the turn of the twentieth century, when the United States was emerging as a great power, Latin American intellectuals assumed ontological distrust of the North in the name of supposedly "spiritual" values as against "material" ones. Paul Groussac and especially José Enrique Rodó ([1900] 1991) occupied themselves in carrying out the task of promoting these spiritual values. In Uruguay, the first Latin American welfare state was established, thanks to the tenacity of José Pedro Varela, the arch defender of "free" education, and later to the action of José Batlle y Ordoñez's government. Following the Mexican Revolution, nationalism, anti-imperialism, socialism, and agrarianism captivated political thought. Two Peruvians, José Carlos Mariátegui on the communist side and Victor Raúl Haya de la Torre on the nationalistic and socialist side persistently exerted influence. Joseph A. Schumpeter (1942) famously predicted that the success of capitalism would generate an intellectual class opposing it; he might as well have predicted that such opposition would spread to countries in which capitalism had not yet taken root. Not until the 1970s did an intellectual—Venezuelan Carlos Rangel—emerge ready to fight a solitary battle against that ideological body united under the curious and contradictory banner of "the left." Our political tradition, joined with ideological confusion and our institutional inheritance, amounted to a mixture of corporatism, mercantilism, socialism, and populism that exalted oligarchies and privileges while it isolated large alienated masses.

The public ended up attributing its own condition to capitalism despite the absence of that system in Latin America and putting its hope in the state, which had replaced the Catholic Church of the nineteenth century and the preceding colonial centuries. Our political action was deeply influence by the developmentalist ideas of Raúl Prebisch, who favored import substitution and the determined action of the state, and later by the theory of dependency advanced by Fernando Henrique Cardoso, who attributed our marginalization to our location on the world's trading periphery and to local oligarchies who served as imperialism's accomplices. First, the Vargases, the Perons, the Lázaro Cárdenas, and the Paz Estenssoros, then later the Velascos and the Castros emerged in all their variants as the product of that tradition of statism. In the 1960s and 1970s, statism reached new heights, bringing a massive wave of nationalizations prompted by an anti-imperialism content to ignore simple statistics showing that—even today in the era of globalization—U.S. investments inLatin America represent only 6 percent of worldwide U.S. investments (Harrison 1997). So strong was the superstition that even the black-economy workers, when voting or voicing their opinions, chose a socialist option. In the 1980s, with the Siles Suazos, the Alan Garcias, the Raúl Alfonsins, and the Daniel Ortegas—precisely when we were making the transition from dictatorship to democracy (or, in the case of Nicaragua, from one dictatorship to another)—the economic chaos, which until then had been ticking away, finally exploded, providing a rationale for the great changes in the 1990s.

Achievements and Failures

Great changes? In some senses yes, in others no. The dynamism of certain reforms in those years cannot be denied. Many governments privatized public companies; reduced tariffs; liberalized various aspects of trade, finance, and agriculture; and adjusted the belts in fiscal and monetary matters. The average inflation rate in the region was 17.7 percent in 1996, which is not bad when compared to the

200 percent in 1991, and income per capita grew each year for almost the entire decade of the 1990s, whereas it had fallen 10 percent in the 1980s. In 1996, foreign investment totaled some $50 billion, a sign of confidence and opening markets. In 1997, of the 500 main companies, 148 were foreign, 285 local, and only 67 state owned; five years earlier, 92 had been state-owned. That only 8 of the 20 largest companies were directly related to natural resources points to a more diversified economy ("500, las mayores empresas" 1996–97). Mexico, Chile, and Argentina have lightened the burden of their governments in more than one sense. In 1982, there were 1,155 public companies in Mexico, and half of all production was by the government. By 1993, $24 billion of public assets had been sold, and the maximum income tax rate had been lowered to 35 percent, which is reasonable by international standards. In Chile, where privatization began much earlier, this process has touched "the untouchables": pensions and health care. More than $40 billion invested in pension funds has boosted savings, expanded the capital market, and benefited the workers, who have seen their savings books record annual interest rates of as much as 14 percent. More than a third of the workers have acquired private health insurance thanks to the government's introducing the option to leave the public health system. Even in Peru, some 100 government companies have been sold, half of which during the nationalization era belonged to Velasco's military regime (Roberts and Lafollette Araujo 1997). Although all these reforms have promoted economic growth during certain periods of the 1990s, they are far from decisive.

Observers tend to judge the quality of the reforms in terms of macroeconomic concepts and statistics. If rates of growth and of inflation, the flow of foreign investment, and the reduced number of government enterprises were the yardsticks by which to measure our progress, Latin America would already be a prosperous continent because since the 1940s its average annual rate of economic growth has been 5 percent, which is greater than the corresponding rate for

Europe. Hyperinflation is a relatively recent phenomenon in our history, as are nationalizations. Between 1900 and 1987, the real gross domestic product (GDP) of Argentina, Brazil, Mexico, Columbia, Chile, and Peru grew an average annual rate of 3.8 percent, more than the corresponding rates for the United States (3.2 percent), for the developed democracies in general (2.9 percent), and for nine Asian economies (3.2 percent). In that period, Brazil had the second highest rate of growth in the world. Factoring in the increase of population, we find that in that period Latin America's average annual rate of growth of GDP per capita was 1.7 percent, almost as great as the corresponding rate for the United States, 1.8 percent (Harrison 1997). It is obvious, however, from Latin America's lagging position and the enormous disparities within its population—in other words, from the quality and the nature of past growth—that we will continue to be underdeveloped. Reliance on macroeconomic indicators gives rise to fallacious conclusions about the development process.

In the past, we Latin Americans were important exporters, but our export activities failed to lay the foundations of genuine development. In the 1950s, 83 percent of the oil bought by the United States came from Venezuela; 95 percent of the coffee, 53 percent of the tin, and 87 percent of the sugar imported by the United States came from Latin America. The world depended on wheat from Argentina, copper from Chile, oil from Venezuela, and tropical products from Brazil (Arciniegas 1958). If exports guaranteed development, Brazil would be a superpower. That country went from exporting goods valued at $136 million in 1965 to exporting goods valued at $136 billion in 1992, of which almost 60 percent consisted of manufactured goods, not raw materials—a direct refutation of the dependency thesis.

Even judging Latin America's reforms of the 1990s from a macroeconomic viewpoint, however, we are left with poor results. In that decade, our economies grew an average annual rate of 3 percent a year, three times faster than in the 1980s but only half as fast as they grew in the 1970s and much slower than East Asia's 8 percent. Only

Chile and El Salvador surpassed that average. In most countries, wages are below the level of the 1980s, and since 1991 unemployment has grown in Mexico, Argentina, and Peru, and the number of people who live on less than a dollar day has increased from 23 percent to 25 percent, whereas in East Asia unemployment has fallen from 17 percent to 13 percent (Sol Linowitz Forum 1997). Peru, whose reforms were praised, has not grown since 1998, and one of every four jobs in the capital has vanished without the market's being able to replace it (Arroyo 2000). Foreign investment in Latin America has reached 20 percent of GDP, which is almost half the ratio for East Asia, but direct investments have been few because investors have preferred highly liquid instruments. Nowadays, receiving investment from abroad is not unusual; even Africa—Nigeria, Ghana, Angola, and of course South Africa—is benefiting from large foreign investments. Yet Latin American exports, even Chile's, still heavily depend on raw materials. It is true that our finances are improving in some cases, but we have acquired more debt than advisable for a healthy economy. The debt of the seven main economies exceeds $600 billion, which is equivalent to almost two and a half times the average of all their exports, even though those exports rose almost 80 percent between 1993 and 1996 (Sol M. Linowitz Forum 1997). Thus, even in macroeconomic terms, our performance has been poor.

Flawed Reforms

The Latin American reforms have suffered from a philosophically fundamental flaw, possibly because they have not been governed by an overall view but by immediate monetary or fiscal needs—in other words, by expediency in the circumstances. This error relates to the confusion between a private economy and a free economy or, better yet, to the divorce between the economy and a government of laws. We have gone from statist economies to private economies, but the state has not ceased to be the determining factor in economic outcomes or in the material fate of the people, often to the detriment of individual rights. We can learn many lessons from this experience. Most important, the *transition* to an open society is quite different from the *creation* of an open society. We liberals who demanded reforms in the 1980s did not anticipate this reality in its full dimensions. When we championed liberalism, we frequently started from a mistaken viewpoint, advocating a free society as if it could be created from emptiness, on virgin territory, like an architectural design. On discovering the quicksand beneath the transition—that is, on discovering that the space is neither empty nor virgin and that within it the existing elements undermine, exhaust, or devour the new—we realized that almost as important as the free society we sought to reach was the route by which we reached it. The transition—the process wherein government yields to the private sector by forsaking mercantilism, privileges, and state enterprises—might easily give way to a subtle, more hypocritical, and almost as injurious state presence dictated by regulationism and the constraints that political power can still attach to private life, despite the state's apparent withdrawal or shrinkage.

Roger Douglas, one of the heroes of New Zealand's transition, has made two points that we Latin American liberals should have considered. First, for him, "the essence of structural reform is the abolishment of privileges," something that is very difficult to achieve because the cost of privileges, being widely dispersed and sometimes invisible to a society, is great in total but small per person and per item (1997). Therefore, the pressure from interest groups seeking to avoid the abolition of their privileges always exceeds the pressure from society as a whole, the overall beneficiary of these reforms. George Reisman (1996) has made a similar point by noting that because a subsidy is much greater per beneficiary than the cost of that subsidy for each taxpayer, lobbyists push hard, whereas the taxpayers do not. Douglas's second observation on transition pertains to the simultaneity of the various reforms, for him an essential condition for success. The economy consists of a network of connections; there is no point in eliminating export subsidies if transport tariffs and regulations are not eliminated, and shipping ports and services are not privatized. What good is it to have fiscal gains as a result of privatization if, instead of reducing taxes or the debt, the government dedicates these gains to exorbitant social expenditures? This very outcome occurred in Argentina during Carlos Menem's administration. By increasing federal and provincial expenses 100 percent, a $6 billion deficit was generated despite the substantial revenue from privatizations. What good is it to relieve the government of its employees if anticapitalist labor legislation prevents the market from reabsorbing those workers, again as happened in Argentina, where Menem's administration bequeathed his successor 15 percent unemployment after having received an unemployment rate of 6 percent from the hands of the unsuccessful Raul Alfonsin? Moreover, if the reforms stop, then the foreign investments, falsely taken to be eternal, will also stop, as recently seen in Peru.

Failing to abolish privileges and failing to effect simultaneous reforms are the two serious flaws in Latin America's reforms. Because of them, we have journeyed toward economies that are more private than before but in many cases not any freer. Where the barriers to the entry of new participants have been insurmountable, the benefits have not been extended to consumers but rather to the government, and numerous visible and invisible regulations have interfered with what Israel Kirzner calls the process of the "discovery of wealth." As Kirzner aptly notes, "the provisions of regulators do not reflect the incentives in the entrepreneurial search for profits" (1995).

The divorce between the economy and the rule of law stems from not understanding that freedom is a political concept before being an economic one and ethical even before political. To suppose that economic reform can be carried out without political reform is to divide the indivisible, to delay indefinitely the emergence of fully free societies. We forget that capitalism in Flanders, Venice, and England was created by means of political processes, by the efforts of merchants to open up their towns for commerce by gaining political concessions from feudal lords and monarchs. Once created, those freer political frameworks generated natural economic consequences. This linkage does not mean that the creation of wealth is a political process. On the contrary, as Franz Oppenheimer (1975) observed, there are only two ways to amass wealth, the economic and the political; the first is the free and rational way, by means of production, and the second is the authoritarian way, by means of violence and expropriation. Still, the economy arises from free human action in a predetermined framework and under specific institutional rules. The attempt to liberalize parts of the economy within an authoritarian political context just as intervening and suffocating as it was previously, with no system of administering impartial justice (a crucial institution for every capitalist process), has resulted in the failure of many of the reforms. Our politicians do not understand economics (Miranda, who did understand some economics, was pleasantly surprised at the end of the eighteenth century to find in the Massachusetts Assembly so many merchants and blacksmiths), and our businessmen do not understand the advantages of doing less politics and more business—although it must be said, to be fair, that their inability is owing in part to the system in which they have had to operate.

Labyrinths of Privilege

One might go on indefinitely enumerating the privileges that have been enthroned or preserved in Latin America's recent reforms. These privileges affect all areas of transaction, from state contracts (in Peru, one of the ministers of the economy has also been one of the government's main contractors) to privatization, commerce, state property, the currency, and pensions.

In privatizing state enterprises, we have with few exceptions granted state-protected monopolies, as in the case of the telephone systems in Mexico, Argentina, and Peru. The quality of service sometimes improved and sometimes did not. The result? The users saw their rates soar and watched with distrust the rapid recovery of investments by the buyers. Cases such as those of Telmex in Mexico or Telefónica in Peru have aroused resentment toward the very idea of privatization and have planted in the public's mind the idea that privatization is not a way to benefit the consumer or to encourage new producers to participate in a market, but the way to grant privileges to a fortunate few and to turn the customers into hostages of a company. The privatization of a Mexican bank through oligopoly—with the government guaranteeing the deposits, limiting foreign participation, and providing protection for last-resort moneylenders—encouraged major corruption. A $68 billion bank rescue of Fobaproa aimed to save some dozen banks, and in Mexico some bankers went so far as to flee from justice. In Peru, as elsewhere, the telephone system was privatized not to benefit the consumer by means of increased competition but rather to allow the state to reap maximum profits—it received $1.8 billion. Instead of distributing property ownership widely, as happened in England and in certain central European countries, privatization in Latin America served to close the tight circle of wealth.

In the arena of trade, the liberalization of recent years has been fraudulent in areas where privileges reign. We saw, for example, how in Guatemala the chicken producers succeeded in getting the government to impose tariffs on the Tyson Company of Arkansas, while at the same time setting import quotas to satisfy peak demand. In Mexico, a series of "compensatory quotas" were set in 1992 by which a tariff of 1,175 percent was levied on goods such as Chinese footwear, and in 1997 apple growers obtained barriers against American Starking from the government. In Brazil, a curious strategy placed extremely high tariffs on computers but extremely low tariffs on dog food. In Columbia, Federcafé, the union of coffee growers and sellers, has had a seat in the executive office, passing regulations that affect its own business.

Similarly discriminating interventionism has affected taxation. Duty-free zones and arbitrary exonerations, such as the maquiladoras or assembly plants, have interfered with the allocation of resources in Mexico, whereas in Argentina the value-added tax was applied selectively so that certain business activities—such as cable, medical insurance, and advertising—escaped the 21 percent tax although it was levied on others. At the end of Menem's term, an interest tax of 15 percent was created to be paid by debt issuers only because the government judged it unfair for them to deduct this interest from their tax statements.

In other areas, even more direct state interference has continued, inasmuch as public companies have continued to operate. In Mexico, Venezuela, and Brazil (in this last country, some 150 companies remained in the state's hands at the end of the 1990s), oil continues to be controlled by the state; and in the "liberal miracle" of Chile, Codelco continues to belong to the government, and the military enjoys a rent from this enterprise protected by the Constitution. What good has it been to Venezuela to generate $250 billion from its oil in the 1980s and 1990s? The absence of a free society and of a market economy has meant that enormous wealth has been wasted.

In currency matters, the examples of privilege are equally numerous. When Venezuela liberalized its exchange rate, producing the inevitable devaluation, oil sales abroad generated more income in Venezuelan currency, and the upshot was increased public spending and inflation. The government could think of nothing better to mitigate the impact of this cash flow than to subsidize private banks that could not invest their excess liquidity because there was no productive activity in which such investment made economic sense.

Even in the area of pensions, where courageous measures have been taken in almost all Latin American countries to move from a distribution system to a capitalization system, one can point to distortions caused by governments that guarantee the existence of clients by requiring them to subscribe to a fund—a privilege unavailable to true entrepreneurs in the free (risky) market.

The Necessary Political Foundations of Genuine Economic Reform

The result of this labyrinthine network of privileges on the South American continent has been a concentration of wealth, which in part explains—with the exception of Chile—why the high rates of economic growth realized in the past have not diminished poverty or advanced the countries as a whole. Sixty percent of the income flows to the top 20 percent of the recipients, and in some cases, such as Peru's, 10 percent of the population controls 70 percent of the wealth, whereas several years ago that top group controlled just 50 percent. Our states thus continue to exemplify, in Bastiat's famous phrase, that "great fiction by which everyone tries to live at everyone else's expense" (qtd. in Leoni 1995)—the rich to gain privileges, the poor to attain what private life has yet to provide them.

The poor deserve praise from liberals for having created the black economy, the popular capitalism that is now usually applauded. This is no minor accomplishment. In countries such as Peru, it represents 38 percent of the GDP and 60 percent of the hours worked, although these same figures reveal the lower productivity that results precisely from an economy's operating on the fringes of the law and behind the state's back. It is true, as Ghersi says in applying Douglass North's analysis of transaction costs to Peru's informal economy, that this lower productivity springs not from cultural factors but from the inefficiency of the legal institutions: for example, to register a tailor's workshop in Peru takes 289 days and $1,200, as well as several bribes, whereas in Tampa, Florida, the same task can be accomplished in three to four hours and by mail (Ghersi 1997). Excessive regulations and the confusion surrounding the regulations have devalued the very idea of law. As Alberto Benegas-Lynch notes, quoting Planiol, "'the inflation of laws translates into a depreciation of the law'" (1999). Each law, each regulation, is a blow to freedom as long as it exalts privileges and discrimination, as happens in Peru, for example, with the conferring of the power of public law on the assembly of university presidents, making them capable of blocking almost completely the entry of new competitors into that market. Most legal regulations, however, take place beyond the premises of the legislature, arising from the administrative bureaucracy, a body that, as indicated by the Public Choice school, is in itself an interest group competing in the mercantilist marketplace. And Latin America's transition has been especially mercantilist in character. We liberals did not anticipate the full significance of the infinite opportunities that the transition from a state economy to a private economy would present for political power and oligarchies, foreign and domestic. We did not foresee very well that after the head of the state economy had been cut off, new ones would sprout, as from the Hydra.

Douglass C. North and Robert Paul Thomas (1973) have demonstrated the impact that secure property rights, contracts, civil responsibility, and the administration of justice had in bringing about economic growth in Europe. Latin America has in many ways still not created the institutions that form the basis of a free society and therefore of a market economy. If "the true objective and design of a government" is "security," as Thomas Paine declared in 1776 (1986), our governments are still not fulfilling their basic mission. The system of administering justice, corrupt and politically servile, continues to be what it was a decade ago: entelechy without content in the best scenario, an active instrument of abuse against citizens in the worst. There have been many studies on the nature of the judicial process in developed capitalist societies. Bruno Leoni has accurately demonstrated that whereas in ancient Greece the law was based on legislation, in Rome it was based on the autonomy of legal advisors, customs, and judicial law. Later Justinian assembled the known laws into codes but incorporated precedents and abundant opinions from legal advisors. "The judicial process," wrote Leoni, "always goes back to individual claims," and "individuals create the law insofar and as soon as they put forward claims that prosper" (1995). The Romans, like the English, believed that law is "discovered" rather than promulgated and that no one in society should be so powerful as to be able to identify his own will with the law of the country. Viewed in this light, law and justice in Latin America are seen to be just the opposite of what they should be. Our justice is not the reflection of the society, but of the power. Instead of inspiring the process of justice, the law and the citizens are its victims, as the daily operation of our legislation demonstrates by ignoring real life—with the black economy being the most flagrant although not the only example. In our justice, politicians and rich businessmen (that is, the powerful) set the standard. This condition explains why the citizens generally distrust the administration of justice, and they have extended that distrust to the whole body of public institutions, creating propitious conditions for militarism or adventurism.

The rule of law is, of course, not the same as democracy. Our democracies can allow alternation in office without protecting individual rights or ceasing to be authoritarian. The Dominican Republic and Venezuela have had more consecutive years of democracy than many other countries in the region without having real protection of economic or even political rights. Costa Rica is without doubt an admirable example of democracy (independence did not come by way of a news item); a symbol of this spirit is José Figueres, who converted the Bella Vista barracks into a museum of fine arts right after the revolution ended in 1948. But Costa Rica's inability to develop substantially during all these years has to do with the absence of truly free and solid institutions. Our leaders can still forever harm the life of the people by decisions made overnight without any consultations.

In the name of supposed human rights, all rights are violated. In the name of "diffuse rights"—those that "belong to everyone, in other words to no one," as Benegas-Lynch (1999) puts it—individuals are deprived of true property rights. Rights can only be concrete, and as Murray Rothbard has maintained, only "human rights that are translated into property rights are valid" (1995) because other rights often run counter to property rights. In the 1980s, Peruvian farmers, rebelling against the collectivist agrarian reform of the previous decade, parceled out 60 percent of the land; in other words, they privatized it. Approximately four million small landholders, however, still had not received property titles in the 1990s. In 1992, Carlos Salinas's administration in Mexico amended the Constitution to allow for private property in the countryside, but a limit of 2,500 hectares was imposed on companies, and the government continued to own the land under Article 27 of the Constitution, according to which "the nation" is the proprietor of land and water. Although more property rights have recently been granted in Mexico than in the past, Article 25 of the constitutional text establishes that the state is the one who "plans, leads, directs, and manages" the economy. No one should be surprised, then, when a large percentage of the investments that arrive in the country take the form of short-term speculations. Moreover, the cacique structure, important in Latin America provinces, has still not been directly attacked in Mexico, which explains, according to economist Oscar Vera, why only 14 percent of all the money CONASUPO distributed for agriculture arrived at its destination (Roberts and Lafollette Araujo 1997). I do not believe that subsidies are a good method for developing the countryside, but this figure reveals how property is controlled by a cacique bureaucracy in the Mexican province and not by citizens with full rights. The absence of true reform in the Mexican political structure allowed the $24 billion allotted by the National Bank of Rural Credit for agricultural subsidies to be used to feed rather than to subdue the guerrilla sedition in the country's southern region.

The superficiality of the poorly named Latin American revolution confirms that political reform must provide the basis for economic reform. The political institutional framework is the environment in which the economy breathes or suffocates. Capitalism's historic roots are a controversial matter, but as a general rule the most successful capitalist countries are those in which a government of laws, often the product of political decentralization and the atomization of power, arose before substantial economic development occurred. It is equally clear that politics obstructs the development of capitalism in authoritarian countries or in those with populist environments. Witness East Asia, where the 1997 crisis can be read as a symptom of weak market economies operating in relatively closed societies. Latin America also presents good examples. The Chilean economy was never as robust and stable or generated as much confidence under Pinochet's regime as under the democracy of the 1990s. The evident corruption, abuse of power, and loss of confidence in Peru today show how a dictatorship, which by definition is the opposite of a rule of law, becomes capitalism's worst enemy. (In another example, the stock market fell five points the day President Fujimori withdrew businessman Baruch Ivcher's Peruvian citizenship in order to expropriate Ivcher's television channel.) When people can be exiled, jailed, tortured, or made to disappear by the state in a country where the law is a docile instrument of political will dedicated to perpetuating a leader, whether civilian or military, then property guarantees and private companies do not provide a body of institutions that can undergird a productive market economy. Instead docile businessmen bow before the government and enter into its corruption.

I blame certain "liberals" for having often been active or passive accomplices of regimes of this caliber, confusing public opinion and marvelously aiding the enemies of freedom. In the Mexico of reforms, President Salinas invited thirty leading businessmen to dinner to request contributions of as much as $25 million a plate for his party. Present were some of the main beneficiaries of monopolistic transfers of companies that were previously state property (A. Oppenheimer 1996). The absence of far-reaching political reforms in Mexico, as in other parts of Latin America, has meant that, despite a widening of the field of private companies and a decrease in state intervention in many areas, economic change has multiplied mercantilist practices and corruption. To some liberals, such as Murray Rothbard (1995), corruption is not bad because it is a "voluntary transaction," but I believe that this attitude is dangerously cynical. Corruption is an arbitrary reassignment of resources; it is almost always an illegal use of funds given to the state by taxpayers and generally implies discriminatory action from a position of political power that favors some and harms others. Borges used to say that the Argentines robbed the state without thinking it a crime because they believed the state was impersonal. Our societies have not yet learned that the state is not an impersonal entity. Neither state decisions nor state expenses are impersonal. In every case, there is a direct relation between these expenses and citizens' property, whether that property takes the form of their lives and freedom or their savings and wealth.

Culture versus Institutions

We liberals will never resolve all our debates. One of them pertains to culture: Does culture influence institutions or vice versa, and which of the two is the key factor in free development? The subject deserves consideration here, albeit tangentially. The first problem arises from the definition of *institutions.* Some observers contrast culture with institutions because they see a clear difference, but others, such as Douglass North, think institutions are "the rules of the game" and include legislation, cultural attitudes, and other forms of restraint on human interaction. "The path to institutional change determines the level of economic opportunity in a society," say North and Thomas (1973). However, North himself (1990) asserts that these formal restraints (regulations) and informal ones (culture) are determined by the market. Others take a completely different view. Lawrence Harrison, although acknowledging that "new policies and institutions are influenced by culture but culture is also influenced by new policies and institutions," maintains that the essential factor is cultural and that the definitive cultural changes that favor economic freedom have not taken place in Latin America (1997). Although Harrison is encouraged by the nearly thirty million Protestants in Brazil and the fifty million in all of Latin America and sees, for example, that the Basque immigration to Chile in the eighteenth century was a determining factor in the progress of that country in the last century as compared to the rest of the region (except for Argentina), his analysis focuses on a fundamental cultural deficit—attitude toward work, merit, frugality, education, ethics, justice, and so forth—that has not yet been remedied.

Rummaging through history, one finds examples of both sorts of influence. The Meiji Revolution in late-nineteenth-century Japan, which spurred the modernization and westernization of that country, was largely a decision made from above. A few decades ago, East Asian countries such as China and Korea exemplified an authoritarian Confucian culture incapable of attaining development; later the East Asian economic explosion, stimulated by the ruling classes, made those countries an example of cultural change generated by institutional decisions because they retained their cultural roots and continued to be partially closed societies. On the other side is the evolution of capitalism in Europe, where emerging merchants and other businessmen succeeded— from below—in gradually bringing the prevailing institutions to reflect their bourgeois culture.

I do not favor an exclusive formula; the process of economic development has been mixed, gradual, and sometimes so replete with shades that it is impossible to determine the proportion of each. Yet one thing is clear: culture alone, if it lacks an institutional correlative in the rule of law, is insufficient; likewise, institutions alone, in a world of anticapitalist culture, are insufficient. The black economy is a magnificent example of an emerging culture that breaks through exclusive and anticapitalist official institutions. This economic sector's development in Latin America began in the 1950s with migrations from the country to the city. After half a century, however, our institutions have yet to reflect this phenomenon appropriately, with the consequences being those that I have already mentioned—the limitations of a black economy, which is an economy of survival more than of development. Similarly, all our formal institutions from the time of independence were dead letters because the beautiful words and desires did not have a cultural and practical counterpart. Isaiah Berlin has observed, "to each stage of social change there corresponds its own type of law, government, religion, art, myth, language, memory" (1976). This observation is manifest in Peru's black economy, which has generated a common law, spontaneous norms, various cultural manifestations such as *"chicha"* music, and even a distinctive politics—all rejected by the traditional political class. It is, therefore, a dual phenomenon, both cultural and institutional, but it still lacks a definite expression in what North (1990) would call the formal institutions. Paradoxically, the *"chicha"* culture, which in many ways embodies a choice for capitalism by the poor, also contains antiliberal atavisms, expressed in many ways, from its adherents' electoral votes to their scorn for the law even when it is "acceptable." Because of the inefficiency and the high cost of the law in this world, its inhabitants have decided to flee from the formal rules in sometimes irrational and paradoxical ways, attacking its own raison d'être—capitalism and the competitive society. Thus, authoritarianism and violence as well as cynicism and a certain degree of resentment are still visible in that culture. According to V. S. Naipaul, "the politics of a country can only be an extension of its view of human relations" (1981). Latin American society still harbors a view of human relations that is incompatible with a liberal civilization, a view apparent in its politics and in other institutions of formal life. Our error is twofold, cultural and institutional, and therefore our adjustment must be twofold. Our formal world has not adapted to our changing social world with its increasingly pro-capitalistic attitudes, nor has our culture adopted the behaviors of a free and civilized society. The process of adjustment must necessarily have an institutional side so that a definitive adaptation also takes place in the culture.

If education is an expression and at the same time an ingredient of culture, our definitive cultural change is far from happening. In this area, with limited exceptions, nothing has been done in recent years in the interest of an open society. Indeed, education has been kidnapped by the state. This capture has nothing to do with money: public expenditure on education in Latin America represents 4.5 percent of the average GDP, higher than Europe's 3.9 percent. It has to do with the appropriateness and philosophy of education. It is believed that education is too valuable to be treated as a commodity and to be subject to market competition, an attitude that demonstrates the poor understanding of what individual freedom is and thereby confuses the matter. By condemning young people to apartheid—a rich minority can pay for private schools, while the rest vegetate in mediocre state education—the government, besides impoverishing education, is strengthening privileges and discrimination in the name of utopian equality and in the name of a false "free" status, which forces those of lesser resources to redistribute income to those above. Timid reforms have been made in the Brazilian state of Minas Gerais, where meetings made up of parents to administer budgets have been allowed; in Columbia, where education vouchers have been granted as an experiment in one province; in Nicaragua, where education vouchers as well as decentralization have been successful; and in Chile, the country that has done the most with the education vouchers, although the state still controls the curriculum. In general, Latin Americans are given an education that, in addition to being of poor quality, is intensely collectivist and fraught with all the prejudices against the individual inherited from the egalitarian tradition. Instead of entering the marketplace knowing from life how important the value of one's own interests are, young people arrive with the notion that "concern for one's own interests is evil, which means to say that man's desire to live is evil" (Rand 1964). Our young people distrust the words *company, gains,* and *profit;* they feel guilty to "care about themselves"—the philosophy that, by the end of his days, even the collectivist Michel Foucault (1984), while studying the individualistic wisdom of the ancients, came to proclaim as a great tradition of Western freedom.

We Latin Americans have still not undertaken the greatest privatization of all, that of political language. We must privatize politics. "Words are signals for ideas, not ideas," according to Herbert Spencer ([1884] 1950). By taking control of political language, the state has been able not only to strip political communication of ideas but also to create a complex network of signals that have trapped the mind of its citizens in an intellectual and ideological spider web with no way of escape. Thus, our reforms have been insufficient also because they have lacked essential intellectual nourishment and an inoculation in the realm of ideas and political language that would immunize the citizens against the collectivists' sophistic viruses and against the hopelessness of that early stage in which the reforms seem only to involve a tremendous cost and no immediate benefit. Owing to this intellectual void, the adversaries of freedom have today turned "neoliberalism" into the great Satan of Latin America. Just as in the mysterious Japanese Kabuki, our political life has become filled with masks that disguise or hide the truth, and we have come to believe that those masks are real faces.

The Prospect

Can we be optimistic about the immediate future in Latin America? "Time wins more converts than Reason," sighed Thomas Paine

([1776] 1986), and he was right, but we have already spent too much time without being converted to the truth. Yes, some things have been left behind for now. Nobody will propose the nationalization of companies in our countries for a long time, and anti-imperialism has been reduced to small circles because our societies admire and emulate the North American example. (An overwhelming reality—annual remittances from our relatives in the United States of some $10 billion to their countries of origin [Harrison 1997]—works against traditional antiyanqui demagoguery.) Of course, the longer-term battle will be fought by the intellectuals, whose influence is enormous. The difference between an idea and a tangible product is that if the latter fails, it ruins its manufacturer or seller, whereas if an idea adopted in politics fails, it ruins the entire society (and the intellectual who created and disseminated it ends up with a professorship in a Yankee university). The "poor morals of the mediocre souls" (Ortega y Gasset [1927] 1974) of our intellectuals preclude great hopes for the members of those circles, but spectacular conversions have occurred in other parts of the world, and efforts should continue to educate our intellectuals. We have some important advantages, the greatest of which is that whereas the advanced societies are aging rapidly, ours are rejuvenating at the same rate. With the present process of capital accumulation, a period in which consumption should undoubtedly be moderate, it will be necessary to make sacrifices and to explain to our societies the usefulness of these sacrifices, but if anyone thinks that the new structures are already in place and that it is just a matter of time, he is mistaken. Many great reforms are still pending in order to ensure development, and in this process a new governing class will be required. Thanks to globalization, with trade growing twice as fast as industrial production, with direct foreign investment of more than $120 billion, and with the nation-state at its weakest point since the Treaty of Westphalia (1648), the thesis of "contagiousness" and "osmosis" has a promising outlook. Still, no one should believe that globalization magically changes countries: it only increases opportunities and determines that if one does not keep his foot in the stirrup, he will soon be thrown back to the Stone Age.

References

Alberdi, Juan Bautista. [1852] 1996. *Bases y puntos de partida para la constitución política de la República Argentina.* Buenos Aires: Edición Plus Ultra.

Arciniegas, Germán. 1958. *Entre la libertad y el miedo.* Buenos Aires: Editorial Sudamericana.

Arroyo, Pilar. 2000. *El contexto socio-económico de las elecciones del 2000.* Lima: Forum Solidaridad Perú.

Benegas-Lynch, Alberto. 1999. *Las oligarquías reinantes.* Buenos Aires: Atlántica.

Berlin, Isaiah. 1976. *Vico and Herder, Two Studies in the History of Ideas.* London: Hogarth.

Douglas, Roger. 1997. The Art of the Possible. In *Liberty.* London.

Fernández, Eduardo. 1999. ¿Sigue vigente el populismo en América Latina? In *¿Sigue vigente el populismo en América Latina?* Caracas: Fundación Pensamiento y Acción.

500, las mayores empresas de América Latina. 1996–97. In *América Economía,* edición anual. Santiago de Chile: Dow Jones.

Ghersi, Enrique. 1997. The Informal Economy in Latin America. *Cato Journal* 17 (spring–summer): 99–108.

Foucault, Michel. 1984. *Le soin de soi.* Paris: Gallimard.

Harrison, Lawrence. 1997. *The Pan-American Dream.* New York: Basic.

Huerta de Soto, Jesús. 1999. Principios básicos del liberalismo. *Revista Hispano Cubana.*

Kirzner, Israel. 1995. *Creatividad, capitalismo, y justicia distributiva.* Madrid: Unión Editorial.

Leoni, Bruno. 1995. *La libertad y la ley.* Madrid: Unión Editorial.

Naipaul, V. S. 1981. *The Return of Eva Peron.* New York: Vintage.

Norris, Floyd. 2000. A Century in the Market: Railroads Once Were the High-Fliers. *International Herald Tribune.*

North, Douglass C. 1990. *Institutions, Institutional Change, and Economic Performance.* Cambridge, Eng.: Cambridge University Press.

North, Douglass C., and Robert Paul Thomas. 1973. *The Rise of the Western World.* Cambridge, Eng.: Cambridge University Press.

Oppenheimer, Andrés. 1996. *Bordering on Chaos.* New York: Little, Brown.

Oppenheimer, Franz. 1975. *The State.* New York: Free Life Editions.

Ortega y Gasset, José. [1927] 1974. *Mirabeau o el político.* Madrid: El Arquero.

Paine, Thomas. [1776] 1986. *Common Sense.* London: Penguin.

Pendle, George. 1976. *A History of Latin America.* London: Penguin.

Rand, Ayn. 1961. *For the New Intellectual.* New York: Signet.

Reisman, George. 1996. *Capitalism: A Treatise on Economics.* Ottawa, Ill.: Jameson.

Roberts, Paul Craig, and Karen Lafollete Araujo. 1997. *The Capitalist Revolution in Latin America.* New York: Oxford University Press.

Rodó, José Enrique. [1900] 1991. *Ariel.* Madrid: Espasa Calpe.

Rothbard, Murray. 1995. *La ética de la libertad.* Madrid: Unión Editorial.

Schumpeter, Joseph A. 1942. *Capitalism, Socialism, and Democracy.* New York: Harper and Row.

Sol M. Linowitz Forum. 1997. *The Americas in 1997: Making Cooperation Work.* Washington, D.C.: Inter-American Dialogue.

Spencer, Herbert. [1884] 1950. *The Man versus the State.* London: Watts.

Véliz, Claudio. 1994. *The New World of the Gothic Fox.* Berkeley: University of California Press.

4

The Individualist Legacy in Latin America

It is often said that the root of Latin America's under-development lies in its statist tradition.[1] That tradition goes as far back as the pre-Columbian states, under which masses of laborers toiled for the benefit of the ruling classes; it includes three centuries of corporatist and mercantilist Ibero-Catholic rule; and it has been compounded in modern times by the elitist independent republics. Through a combination of institutional arrangements set in place at various times by the governing cliques and cultural values transmitted from generation to generation, Latin America's tradition weighs so heavily against ideas of limited government, the rule of law, and personal responsibility that it would seem that an almost determinist view is justified in regarding liberty as beyond the region's reach.

Yet from the days when Indians in parts of Central America and Mexico used cacao seeds as money to the present-day informal economy, the instinct of the Latin American people is no different from that of the rest of the human species. Nothing suggests that the native cultures, either in their precolonial or in their mestizo forms, could not have responded creatively and successfully to the incentives of liberty had they been allowed to operate under less-oppressive conditions.

An individualist spirit has sought to manifest itself in Latin America in all historical periods. This legacy goes as far back as the family units that worked their own land and exchanged goods in ancient times, moving from them to the Jesuits of the School of Salamanca who discovered the monetary causes of inflation and the subjective nature of value at the very time when Spain colonized Latin America in the sixteenth century, and from them to the informal (black-market) economy that represents a contemporary and inventive response by the people to the state's illegitimacy. Inbetween these episodes stand landmarks such as the mid-sixteenth-century rebellion of Gonzalo Pizarro, the 1812 liberal Constitution of Cádiz, Spain, the ideas that inspired the Latin American independence struggle, the brilliant Argentinean three-quarter century that flowed from Juan Bautista Alberdi's vision, and a few post–World War II intellectuals who went against the current.

Trade and Property in Ancient Times

Despite the limits on communication imposed by the absence of pack animals and by the fact that the wheel had not yet been discovered in the area, trade occurred in all three of the great pre-Columbian civilizations—the Incas, the Aztecs, and the Mayas (who used the wheel only in toys). The powerful bureaucracies established in ancient Latin America used the tradition of commerce for their own purposes and to a large extent curtailed mercantile private initiative precisely because they appreciated its significance.

Trade played an important part in making possible the loose confederate organization of the Maya culture that flourished in the Yucatán Peninsula and the surrounding areas, with no permanent political center, but rather a system of city-states, Tikal being the best known, among which hegemonic influence shifted. In fact, long before the classic period of Maya civilization, taken to have started in the third century A.D., trade was a mainstay at locations such as Chiapa de Corzo, Abaj Takalik, El Baúl, and Chalchuapa (James 2001). Thanks to commerce, the communities of the coast were later fed not by the agricultural lands in their immediate vicinity, but by the interior hinterlands, where they obtained food as well as textiles and other goods. When the Europeans arrived, the Maya city-states had long waned, but the descendants of that civilization were well acquainted with the notion of exchange.

A commercial tradition was also strong in Mexico. Before Tenochtitlán established itself as the undisputed capital of what is known as the Aztec Empire, that city-state coexisted with Tlatelolco, an entirely mercantile center. Through trade, Tlatelolco developed a class of merchants and entrepreneurs (Garraty and Gay 1972). Tenochtitlán was naturally jealous of those merchants, who traded in valuable commodities (James 2001). Despite political centralization, trade continued to be a feature of daily life once Tenochtitlán had become the imperial nerve center.[2] The *pochtecas* specialized in long-distance commerce and supervised markets in the Valley of Mexico. The Mexicas of the capital traded with the surrounding areas, exchanging water-intensive products (the city stood on a huge lagoon) for wood and stone. Although the empire was divided between the ruling class and a great mass of laborers, the merchants numbered as many as ten thousand (Wolf 1999). They even had special law courts. Their activities were not spared many of the controls suffered by other types of activities, but they still constituted a culture of exchange in which mutual benefit, not simple predation, was the guiding principle. From that exchange flowed elementary concepts of money, with the use of gold, zinc, and other media. Trade also occurred at the other end of the region, in the Andes. The Incas went a long way toward eliminating it, precisely because it was a tradition. Important cultures had surfaced in what is known today as Peru long before the Incas. The people of the Tiahuanaco culture, born around A.D. 500 in the mountains of southern Peru, traded intensely with the coast and even with Central America. Before the Inca Empire came into being, when the Inca kingdom was but one among many others, trade continued to be a part of life in the Andes. It was an activity that engaged many women, whose presence in the market was particularly visible. One Inca, Túpac Yupanqui, is remembered for having ordered free passage across the land to those who chose to take part in commerce. Many of the Inca's decisions were announced in the marketplace (Cabello de Balboa 1951).

Because the people had no written language, scant evidence exists of just how intense trade was before the Inca Empire and how much of it survived until Spain conquered South America, but notarial records of early colonial times attest to the Indians' acquaintance with contract and commerce despite the stifling controls put in place by the Inca Empire. Testimonies given by Indians in local Peruvian communities to Spanish inspectors in the sixteenth century clearly speak of trade. The records also show *kurakas* (local chiefs) providing labor to the Spaniards in exchange for a fee, using traditional social customs (Spalding 1973). The *kuraka* received raw cotton from the Spaniards and distributed it to the Indians under his jurisdiction. He then sold the finished cloth to the Spaniards for cash payment. By the mid–sixteenth century, the Indians were already diverting part of their labor for the production of goods for the Spanish market. By the eighteenth century, not only *kurakas* but also the wealthier members of Indian society in general traded their possessions in the Spanish markets for goods they then sold to fellow Indians. An entire class of merchants called *principales* stocked the shops that they set up in their communities with European commodities bought from Spanish merchants.[3] Although the incorporation of Indians into the Spanish market owes much to the dislocation of traditional social norms caused by colonial rule, the Indian society's immediate response to the market attests to traditions of trade.

Another element of individualism, apart from commerce, also existed in the ancient Andes. Between the time of the Tiahuanaco culture's decline and the emergence of the Inca Empire, a political eclipse occurred during which the people went back to their small land-based clans, which employed a form of private property. Each *ayllu* consisted of one or more families claiming to descend from some remote godlike ancestor.[4] The families owned the land, which the chief distributed. The houses in which they lived, as well as the orchards, belonged to them. So did their tools. Although the chief wielded power over the community, he had obligations, including the protection of private property. Differences in wealth inevitably developed between the communities, which led to war (Vargas Llosa 1994). The *kuraka* represented the kindred members of his community, and the community members, in exchange for favors and labor they were not actually obliged to supply, received services such as the settlement of disputes, the enforcement of claims by the weaker members, and the conduct of rituals. Evidence of many disputes between *kurakas* and their local kinsmen indicates how strongly the members of the community felt about authority's invasion of their sphere (Guamán Poma de Ayala [1615] 1987).

Anyone who visits a market fair among the Indian communities of the Andes, southern Mexico, or Guatemala will detect a powerful spirit of trade among peoples who in many ways remain remote from the mainstream of Western culture. One has only to see how peasants have parceled out 60 percent of the land collectivized by agrarian reform in Peru to recognize the heritage of ancient times, when the communities used to parcel out the land among the families and individuals who subsequently became its owners. Notable, too, are the arts of pottery and weaving, which Indians practice with as much ingenuity today as in centuries long past and strive to place in the local or international market. So among the Indians who came to be organized in vast empires under the Aztecs and the Incas, and in powerful city-states in the case of the Mayas, the spirit of the individual was not dead. Imperial power did much to coerce that spirit into subservience, but it did not eliminate the continuation of that spirit as an element of the cultural heritage.

Rebellion and Sound Economics in Colonial Times

The conquest of South America was marked by tensions over property and autonomy between the conquerors and the Spanish monarchy that chartered them. The outcome was determined early on, when the independent-minded first wave of conquistadores put up an ultimately unsuccessful fight against the metropolitan power in defense of private property and government by consent. That the conquistadores exploited the native population and burdened the laborers with large tributes does not detract from the point that principles of limited government and private property emerged under significant players' leadership. These players constitute an important precedent. Chief among the rebels was Gonzalo Pizarro, the brother and political heir of Francisco Pizarro.

In the mid-1540s, the Spanish monarchy established direct control over the colonies and enacted laws limiting the conquistadores' estates (Muro Orejón 1945). The ensuing conflict in Peru saw the emergence of an ideologically motivated movement under Gonzalo Pizarro. Major intellectual voices justified their sedition against absolutism with ideas of government by consent and private property. The rebels based a good part of their claims on St. Thomas Aquinas's natural-rights doctrine and on the medieval Spanish legal codes known as Las Siete Partidas, which echoed Justinian's codification of Roman jurisprudence. Monarchical absolutism had swept away such notions in the Iberian world, but the moral and intellectual force of such principles remained sufficient to send shivers down the king's spine. Gonzalo Pizarro's men were well aware of the commotion provoked by the local communities that had revolted against taxes and other limitations of their freedoms in Castile before the rise of the unified Spanish monarchy. Moreover, even within the realm of rigid scholastic doctrine, legal and moral voices in Spain sought to place government under the rule of higher principles. The king's reaction to Pizarro's rebellion therefore aimed to prevent further cracks in the edifice of absolutism as much as to retain control of the colonies.

In documents such as *Representación de Huamanga,* the manifesto of the rebellion, as well as in letters to the king, Gonzalo Pizarro and his men stated that defending property and questioning laws that had been passed without consultation was not tantamount to disloyalty (Lohmann Villena 1977). In warning that they would "obey but not comply" with the laws, they sought to avoid opening themselves to the accusation of high treason, but they also resorted to the defense of moral principle against government. The rebels, who met cruel deaths (and inflicted some, too), were the unwitting heirs of a tradition vested in the local villages of Spain that traditionally had resisted the king's authority. In less-obvious ways, they also remind us of the Saracens, who had ruled Iberia with a liberal hand and whose scientific energy and enterprise still infused that part of the world when the unified Christian monarchy that expelled the Moors (Muslims) undertook the conquest of the Americas.

A much more systematic and profound (if equally unheeded by the political authorities) contribution to the individualist spirit in the sixteenth century was the School of Salamanca, a group of Jesuit and Dominican scholastic thinkers now considered forerunners of the Austrian school of economics of the nineteenth and twentieth centuries.[5] They did not question the divine nature of the Hapsburg monarch; indeed, they provided the theological justification for it. Still, those associated with the School of Salamanca introduced common sense into the theological perspective on worldly matters and debunked many misconceptions regarding the value of goods, the role of money, and taxation. They based their beliefs on natural law as developed by Thomas Aquinas (who was influenced by Aristotelian philosophy) a few centuries earlier (Huerta de Soto 1999).

Although their teachings did not shape public policy in Spain or therefore in Latin America, where in practice scholasticism meant the theological justification of colonial oppression, the Salamancan scholars constitute a venerable legacy of sound economic thinking. The first scholars "to grasp the role of commerce and trade in bring-

ing about an interdependent world based upon law and consent"
(Novak 1990, 45) remind us that a very different type of choice might
have been made and that lack of reasonable ideas is not to blame for
the type of colonial legacy by which Latin America in many ways
remains shackled.

Long before the Austrians, the School of Salamanca discovered
the subjective nature of value, under which no good in the market
has an objective value that can be determined by the authorities or
by any other outsider. Value, as Diego de Covarrubias y Leyva, Luis
Saravia de la Calle, Jerónimo Castillo de Bovadilla, and others stated, has to do with each individual's "esteem" of a good. The only
way to establish the "just price"—that medieval obsession—therefore is to let supply and demand (the interplay of "esteems") do their
work. Prices are not determined by costs, which (including wages)
are themselves prices, but by the public in a competitive exchange
environment. "Only God" knows what the "just price" is.[6]

Alejandro Chafuén (1986) has aptly described many other contributions made to the capitalist ethos by the School of Salamanca.
Francisco de Vitoria, a leading scholar, denounced the slavery of Indians as running contrary to natural law; Domingo de Soto and Tomás
de Mercado criticized common ownership; Juan de Mariana justified
killing tyrants because they violated law and consent, and he asked
for both moderate taxes and a reduction of public spending; Martín
de Azpilcueta, Luis de Molina, and Diego de Covarrubias y Leyva
understood the monetary causes of inflation, a major topic at a time
when the importation of Latin American bullion was affecting prices
in Europe; and, finally, Fray Felipe de la Cruz and others, though not
going so far as to accept the concept of interest, which was an anath-
ema at the time, justified the discounting of bills of exchange.

The School of Salamanca (not all its figures were actually associated with that university) expresses an old tradition of capitalist thought in the Spanish world that ruled Latin America. It was
eclipsed by the spirit of the Counter Reformation, which was so

prevalent that these scholastics themselves were part of it. Their valuable economic lessons thus amounted to academic speculation while real policy was reserved for everything they so lucidly attacked.

Liberalism in Republican Times

The independence movement of the late eighteenth and early nineteenth centuries also contained some genuine expressions of liberty.

Free trade was one of them. The Spanish monopoly was an essential target of the Creole revolt. Being able to trade with England, France, Holland, and other places was a major aspiration. Additional forms of government intervention were also severely questioned. The ideas of Rousseau and other collectivists of the Enlightenment were not the only ones feeding Latin Americans' imagination. The French Physiocrats, with their message of minimal government direction and their belief that progress came from the freedom of individuals to multiply the resources of nature, also had a strong impact, as did the American Founding Fathers, especially for leaders such as Francisco de Miranda. Calls for abolishing taxes and duties were no less powerful than the defense of free trade.

Civic engagement at the local level during the independence struggle was symptomatic of grassroots efforts to decentralize power. These efforts were not like New England town-hall meetings, but the municipalities were focal points of citizen discussion and participation and of efforts at liberation from the centralized colonial structures. Civic associations—including religious groups, especially Masonic clubs—took active roles in creating local networks for the independence struggle. They constituted an embryonic form of civil society that the subsequent kidnapping of the independent republic by military caudillos tragically stifled.

The independence movement was a complex mix of liberal and conservative tendencies. The 1812 Constitution, signed by Spanish politicians and a number of Latin American delegates in the Spanish city of Cádiz under Napoleon's occupation, became a symbol of liberalism for the independence movements. Yet this ideal on the part of some participants coexisted with a conservative distrust of liberalism on the part of many Creoles, for whom French influence in Spanish affairs actually became a reason for breaking ties with the metropolis. Thus, two contradictory forces were present at the very birth of the Latin American republics. The political struggles that ensued and the privileged position enjoyed by the elites who led the independence effort ensured that both sides, liberals and conservatives, became tainted with the same evils: authoritarianism and mercantilism. The effect was to give rise to very limited republican institutions (José Martí called them "theoretical republics") that did not take root among the people—a major cause of the state's illegitimacy, which would spark later revolutions. Still, liberal ideas were a real presence at the start of the independence movement, and some leading figures' liberal beliefs were genuine.

Amid the chaos and the furor of Latin America's nineteenth century, one story speaks to us of a significant degree of civilization: Argentina's relatively limited government under its 1853 Constitution, which laid the foundation for some seven decades of economic expansion.

The name of Juan Bautista Alberdi, a leading member (together with Domingo Faustino Sarmiento) of the remarkable Argentine "generation of 1837," has been lost amid the names of the more colorful, larger-than-life despots of his time (including that legendary tyrant José Manuel Rosas, who ruled from Buenos Aires until 1852). Alberdi's book *Bases y puntos de partida para la organización de la República Argentina,* published in 1852 (1996), served as a guideline for the Constitution of 1853. It reflected to a large extent his belief, influenced by the American Revolution and the U.S. Constitution, that government's essential role was the protection of life and property, that federalism was the best possible compromise between central and local government, and that free trade was the engine of progress. An obsession with populating the country and encouraging European immigration was salient alongside his admiration of Adam Smith, David Hume, the French Physiocrats, and the *Federalist Papers* (his weakness for Bentham and others tainted his liberal persuasion with utilitarianism). Under leaders able to give some practical meaning to these constitutional principles (unlike what was happening elsewhere in the continent), Argentina managed to narrow the scope of its government's powers and to remove obstacles to both capitalist endeavor and voluntary association. The degree of free enterprise included, for example, provision for commercial banks to issue their own notes in the 1880s, something unthinkable today (Benegas Lynch 1986).

Because of institutional reforms and no doubt also a cultural predisposition on the part of many European immigrants, the country experienced the second highest rate of economic growth and enjoyed the greatest rate of foreign investment per capita in the world during the latter part of the nineteenth century. From 1892 to 1913, the wages and income in real terms for rural and industrial workers were higher than in Switzerland, Germany, and France. In 1910, the volume of Argentina's exports exceeded those of Canada and Australia (Benegas Lynch 1990). By the 1920s, its economy was well ahead of many western European economies, and a solid middle class constituted the backbone of society; in 1928, its GDP per capita was the twelfth greatest in the world (Grondona 1999) (still less than half that of the United States, however). Its cultural offerings were no less admired than its economic progress.

Later events, with the rise of populism, led Argentina along a very different path, however, indicating that despite the important inroads that capitalism made in that country, the phenomenon did not cut deep enough, especially in the pampas and the countryside, to become part of a permanent culture.[7] To be sure, authoritarianism never really ceased to exist and political participation was restricted under the 1853 Constitution, but the visionary "generation of 1837" has to be credited with infusing the political atmosphere and with shaping events in a manner that might have evolved into something more sustained and widespread.

Today's Individualist Survivors

For proof that Latin Americans are the same as others in their instinctive pursuit of self-interest through enterprise and exchange, no contemporary phenomenon speaks more eloquently than the informal ("underground") economy. It should be called the "survival economy" because it refers to the millions of people all over the world who carve out an existence for themselves outside of the law simply because doing business legally—everything from obtaining licenses and incorporating a small firm to complying with local and central government regulations—is expensive and time-consuming or impossible. The legal system offers no guarantees to those who are not close to the political machinery that decides the fate of any type of enterprise.

It is estimated that the informal economy amounts to $9 trillion worldwide, nearly as large as the U.S. economy.[8] Although all nations have an informal economy, in rich countries it represents an average of 14 percent of all the goods and services provided, whereas in underdeveloped countries it represents at least twice that much (in sub-Saharan African countries the figure is 54 percent).[9] Because informality means lack of predictable property rights and enforcement mechanisms, insecurity and risk are very high in the informal economy. Without access to formal credit, insurance, and other institutions, productivity is low. The informal economy is a labor-intensive world in which the costs of illegality—from very high interest rates on informal credit and insurance to the absence of enforceable tort law—hold down productivity and growth. In most underdeveloped countries, the proportion of workers involved in providing informal goods and services is large. The operation of this economy, however, means quite simply the survival of the poor.

Housing, transport, manufacturing, retail commerce, and other activities to which informal producers devote their time represent approximately 60 percent of all hours worked in Peru (Ghersi 1997). Informal employment accounts for more than 50 percent of the working population in Mexico and for 40 percent of wage earners in Argentina (Ricci 2002), and it involves more Brazilians than the combined number of people in the public sector and in formal industry in that country (Neves 1999).

The informal economy has created not only a parallel economy but also a sort of parallel culture. By the 1980s and 1990s, it had become fashionable to state that the informal economy is not simply a spectacle of land grabs, bloody conflicts among shantytown neighbors, messy street vending, unsafe and pollution-prone public transport vehicles, and disloyal tax evasion, but rather proof of an entrepreneurial spirit among the poor that represents the promise of vibrant development. Latin America elites discovered with amazement (or was it horror?) that the poor, just like the rest, actually like to own property, produce goods and services privately, exchange them by contract rather than by command, and enjoy the fruits of their labor. Every politician and commentator praised the inventiveness, entrepreneurial spirit, productive potential, survival instincts, organizational skills, and cultural achievements of the "informals," as they began to call the poor. These politicians and analysts were unaware that the underground economy had been noticed in other parts of the poor world much earlier and that it had been lauded as the social cushion preventing revolution in other regions. As early as 1971, anthropologist Keith Hart had delivered an address in which he spoke of the informal economy in some African nations as "a means of salvation" that allows people "denied success by the formal opportunity structure" to "increase their incomes" (Hart 1973, 67). Even earlier, both Latin American and U.S. researchers had conducted studies in

Latin American urban squatter settlements, with results that allowed scholars in the mid-1970s to identify customary rules and norms arising out of informal arrangements and providing a certain security, justice, and organization to urban dwellers.[10]

The informal economy is hardly a new development: the rise of the West in centuries past took place in exactly the same way, with millions of people producing and exchanging goods and services under spontaneous rules of the game that developed according to expanding needs and in circumvention of the authorities who laid down the onerous, burdensome, and elitist laws. In Latin America, too, the tradition is old. Most of the trade conducted under colonial rule was illegal, and urban squatting existed as early as the sixteenth century. When, centuries later, the Portuguese monarch fled to Brazil after the invasion of Portugal by Napoleon's army, thus paving the way for a peaceful independence, one of the most important measures of economic liberalism was to authorize the open sale of any commodity in the streets and door to door (Viotti da Costa 1975, 51).

In Latin America, despite ritual gestures in favor of the informal economy, such as distributing property titles or deeds that signify "ownership," but not real, fungible property in practice, the legal sector continues to exclude the "other" by imposing barrier after barrier to entry. Still, the embryonic capitalism that one can identify in the informal economy—a spirit of enterprise, contract, and exchange—attests that Latin America's corporatist, mercantilist, and authoritarian legacy has not wiped out the potential for a free society and therefore for real development. Yes, the perpetuation of impediments to free enterprise has ingrained a culture of disregard for the law that at first sight suggests major difficulties for the rise of fully developed free-market capitalism under the rule of law. Nevertheless, the unprejudiced observer cannot help but see the resilience of individualism under perpetual institutional oppression.

In fact, the informal economy attests precisely to an individualist legacy that has coexisted, in diminished but real form, with the dominant culture through the centuries. The individualist legacy is dual. One dimension is academic and intellectual, extending all the way from the School of Salamanca at the time when Latin America was an Iberian colony, to the handful of Latin American intellectuals who set out as early as the 1970s to debunk contemporary myths, among them Carlos Rangel in Venezuela and the pioneers of the Francisco Marroquín University in Guatemala, who have since inspired a growing group of writers and academic centers. The other dimension is practical, with ancient roots, traceable even under the suffocating states of the pre-Columbian world, in the customary behavior of native inhabitants who sought to obtain the elements of subsistence from nature and from social cooperation of various kinds. This legacy continues to stare in the face anyone who goes to Latin America. It is the daily struggle of ordinary men and women who survive by means of clandestine property and enterprise.

Notes

1. The term *Latin America* is an invention of nineteenth-century French sociologists. It has become widely accepted, except in Spain, where the terms *Spanish America* and *Ibero America* are usually preferred.

2. Among the numerous tribes of the Valley of Mexico, the Mexica emerged as the dominant force. Their "Triple Alliance" with the Acolhuaque and the Tepaneca facilitated an expansion beyond the valley. Numerous alliances and subordinated tribes constituted what is known as the "Aztec" Empire, a less pervasive and "imperial" type of organization than that of the Incas (Gibson 1964).

3. Archivo Nacional del Perú, Sección Histórica, Derecho Indígena, Cuaderno 491.

4. Fray Domingo de Santo Tomás ([1560] 1951) equates *ayllu* with lineage or family.

5. Carl Watner (1987) refers to their constituting a "libertarian tradition."

6. This quote is by the Spanish Jesuit Juan de Lugo (Huerta de Soto 1999, 105).

7. Mariano Grondona (1999) argues that his country, Argentina, is the only one in the world to have underdeveloped itself—that is, to have attained a situation of development and then to have descended into underdevelopment.

8. For a survey of the underground economies of 110 countries, see Schneider 2002.

9. These figures come from an address given by Professor Friedrich Schneider cited in Thatcher 2002, 418.

10. One case study was conducted in some barrios of Caracas, Venezuela, and published in Karst, Schwartz, and Schwartz 1973.

References

Alberdi, Juan Bautista. [1852] 1996. *Bases y puntos de partida para la organización de la República Argentina.* Buenos Aires: Plus Ultra.

Benegas Lynch, Alberto. 1986. *Fundamentos de análisis económico.* Buenos Aires: Abeledo-Perrot.

———. 1990. Rediscovering Freedom in Argentina. In *Fighting the War of Ideas in Latin America,* edited by John Goodman and Ramona Morotz-Baden, 121–28. Dallas: National Center for Policy Analysis.

Cabello de Balboa, Miguel. 1951. *Miscelánea Antártica.* Lima: Instituto de Etnología.

Chafuén, Alejandro. 1986. *Christians for Freedom.* San Francisco: Ignatius.

Garraty, John, and Peter Gay, eds. 1972. *The Columbia History of the World.* New York: Harper and Row.

Ghersi, Enrique. 1997. The Informal Economy in Latin America. *Cato Journal* 17 (spring–summer): 99–108.

Gibson, Charles. 1964. *The Aztecs under Spanish Rule: A History of the Indians of the Valley of Mexico 1519–1810.* Stanford, Calif.: Stanford University Press.

Grondona, Mariano. 1999. *Las condiciones culturales del desarrollo económico: Hacia una teoría del desarrollo.* Buenos Aires: Ariel-Planeta.

Guamán Poma de Ayala, Felipe. [1615] 1987. *Nueva crónica y buen gobierno.* Madrid: Historia.

Hart, Keith. 1973. Informal Income Opportunities and Urban Employment in Ghana. *Journal of Modern African Studies* 11, no. 1 (March): 61–89.

Huerta de Soto, Jesús. 1999. Principios básicos del liberalismo. *Revista Hispano Cubana* 4 (May–September). http://www.hispanocubana.org/.

James, N. 2001. *Aztecs and Maya: The Ancient Peoples of Middle America.* Charleston, S.C.: Tempus.

Karst, Kenneth L., Murray L. Schwartz, and Audrey J. Schwartz. 1973. *The Evolution of the Law in the Barrios of Caracas.* Los Angeles: Latin American Center, University of California.

Lohmann Villena, Guillermo. 1977. *Ideas jurídico-políticas en la rebelión de Gonzalo Pizarro: La tramoya doctrinal del levantamiento contra las leyes nuevas en el Perú.* Valladolid, Spain: Seminario Americanista, Secretariado de Publicaciones de la Universidad.

Muro Orejón, Antonio, ed. 1945. *Las leyes nuevas, 1542–1543: Reproducción de los ejemplares existentes in la Sección de Patronato del Archivo General de Indias.* Seville: Sevilla.

Neves, Francesco. 1999. Making Do. *Brazzil* 160 (June). http://www.brazzil.com/.

Novak, Michael. 1990. *This Hemisphere of Liberty: A Philosophy of the Americas.* Washington D.C.: American Enterprise Institute.

Ricci, Rudá. 2002. *A economia política da Argentina.* http://www.ts.ucr.ac.cr/~historia/mod-his/arge-ecopol.htm.

Santo Tomás, Domingo de. [1560] 1951. *Lexicón o vocabulario de la lengua general del Perú.* Lima: Instituto de Historia.

Schneider, Friedrich. 2002. *Size and Measurement of the Informal Economy in 110 Countries Around the World.* http//rru.worldbank.org/documents/informal_economy.pdf.

Spalding, Karen. 1973. *Kurakas* and Commerce: A Chapter in the Evolution of Andean Society. *Hispanic American Historical Review* 53, no. 4 (November): 586–88.

Thatcher, Margaret. 2002. *Statecraft: Strategies for a Changing World.* New York: Harper-Collins.

Vargas Llosa, Alvaro. 1994. *The Madness of Things Peruvian.* New Brunswick, N.J.: Transaction.

Viotti da Costa, Emília. 1975. The Political Emancipation of Brazil. In *From Colony to Nation: Essays on the Independence of Brazil,* edited by A. J. R. Russell-Wood. Baltimore: Johns Hopkins University Press.

Watner, Carl. 1987. "All Mankind Is One": The Libertarian Tradition in Sixteenth-Century Spain. *Journal of Libertarian Studies* 8, no. 2 (summer): 293–309.

Wolf, Eric R. 1999. *Envisioning Power.* Berkeley and Los Angeles: University of California Press.

Index

AFJP Máxima, 8
Alberdi, Juan Bautista, 22, 28–29, 54, 62–63
Alborta, Freddy, 8
Almendros, Néstor, 17
American stock market, 23–24
anticapitalist culture and institutions, 46
anticapitalist labor legislation in Argentina, 35
apartheid in education system, 47
Arbenz, Jacobo, 11
Arciniegas, Germán, 23
Argentina
    Alberdi's legacy in, 22, 28–29, 54, 62–63
    descending into underdevelopment, 63–64, 67n7
    social welfare from privatization profits, 35
Aristidio, 11
Arzuaga, Javier, 13–14
Aspiazú, Iñake de, 14
authoritarian caudillos in Latin America, 24, 30, 36
Azpilcueta, Martín de, 60
Aztec Empire, 54, 55, 67n2

Banderas, Antonio, 10

banks, privatization of, 37
Baroque art as symbol of Counter-Reformation Spain, 26
Bases and Points of Departure for the Political Constitution of the Argentine Republic (Alberdi), 22, 28–29, 62–63
Bases y puntos de partida para la organización de la República Argentina (Alberdi), 22, 28–29, 62–63
Bastiat, Frédéric, 39
Batista regime, Che Guevara compared to, 3–4
Batlle y Ordóñez, José, 29
Bay of Pigs invasion of Cuba, 16
Benegas-Lynch, Alberto, 40, 42
Berlin, Isaiah, 46
Betancourt, Ernesto, 19
Betto, Frei, 9–10
black economy, 39, 46, 54, 64–67
Boétie, Etienne de la, 3
Bolivia, 21
Bourbon reforms, 27
Bustos, Ciro, 21

La Cabaña prison, 12–14
cacique structure, 42
capitalism
    black economy as, 39, 46, 54, 64–67

capitalism (*cont.*)
  bringing along the culture and institutions, 46–47
  contingent success of, 29
  Guevara's accusation of Soviet, 19
  Latin Americans's blaming of, 29–30
  laws of government as precursor to, 43
  prospects for, 49
  and Salamancan scholars, 27–28, 54, 59–61
  See also market economy
capitalist brand, Che Guevara as, 7–10
Cardoso, Fernando Henrique, 30
Castañeda, Jorge, 14
Castillo de Bovadilla, Jerónimo, 28, 60
Castro, Fidel, 10, 12, 17, 24
Catalán, El, 12
caudillismo governments in Latin America, 24, 29, 30
Chafuén, Alejandro, 60
Chávez, Hugo, 24
Che Guevara cult members, 1–2, 8–9, 9–10
"chica" culture, 46
China, 19
Christians, Guevara's execution of, 14
City Lights Books, San Francisco, Calif., 9
Ciutat, Francisco, 16
civic engagement and civic associations, 61
Codelco, 38
collectivist rationalism in Latin America, 25–26, 47–48
colonization of Latin America, 4, 26–28, 53, 58–61
commerce in seventeenth century, 27
Comtian positivism, 28
concentration camps, 16, 17
Congo expedition (1965), 21
Constitution of 1812 as symbol of liberalism, 62

Constitution of 1853 in Argentina, 22, 62–63
Constitution of Cádiz, Spain, 54
constitutions, constant changes to, 25–26
constructivist rationality, 28
corruption, 40–41, 44
Corzo, Petro, 12, 14
Costa Vázquez, Jaime, 12
Counter-Reformation Spain, 26, 28–29, 61
counterrevolutionary, broad definition of, 16
Covarrubias y Leyva, Diego de, 28, 60
Creoles, independence movement and, 62
Cruz, Felipe de la, 60
Cuba, 16, 18–20
Cuban independence movement, 16
Cuban missile crisis, 18
Cuban police state, 15–16
cultural deficit, 45
culture and institutions (or institutions and culture), 44–48
culture of informal economy, 65–66

Dargis, Manohla, 9
Daroussenkov, Oleg, 19
Debray, Régis, 21
debt, 33
decentralized, individual-based rights, 5, 53–54
  See also individual and individualism
democracy, rule of law versus, 41
Dheisheh refugee camp, West Bank, Israel, 9
dictatorships in Latin America, 24
Douglas, Roger, 34–35
D'Rivera, Paquito, 14

East Asia, 32–33, 43, 45
Echevarría, 11

economic growth, requirements for, 40

economic growth in Argentina, 63

economic reform, political foundation for, 34–36, 39–44

economics of Latin America
    expediency policy as flaw in, 33–34
    institutions and culture, 44–48
    interest groups and their privileges, 34, 36–39
    liberalization of trade with privileges for wealthy, 37–38, 49
    mercantilist marketplace, 40, 44, 56
    pensions, 31, 38–39
    prospects for improvements, 48–50
    reforms with mixed results, 30–33
    Salamancan scholars's influence on, 27–28, 54, 59–61
    subsidies, 34, 35, 38, 42
    tariffs, 37–38
    trade and property in ancient times, 54–57
    See also capitalism; market economy; privatization

economy of survival, black economy as, 46

education, state-sponsorship of, 47

educational reform, 47–48

El Nuevo Herald, 14

Ernesto (Gadea), 11

federalism, Alberdi's belief in, 63

Federcafé, 38

Fernándes-Zayas, Marcelo, 12

Ferreyra, Chichina, 10

Fobaproa bank rescue, 37

forced labor camps in Cuba, 16–17

foreign investments, 31, 33, 49–50, 63

Foucault, Michel, 48

Francisco Marroquín University, Guatemala, 67

freedom, political leading to economic, 35–36, 40, 41–42

freedom or oppression, clarity from narrowing field to, 3–4

French Physiocrats, 61

Fujimori, Alberto, 24

Gadea, Hilda, 11

Gavi, Philippe, 18

George A. Romero's Land of the Dead (*New York Times* review), 9

Ghersi, Enrique, 39

globalization, 49–50

government
    caudillismo governments, 24, 29, 30
    laws of government as precursor to capitalism, 43
    objectives over laws formula for, 24
    privatization with government control, 34–36, 37, 39–40
    See also rule of law

Granado, Alberto, 7–8

Grondona, Mariano, 67n7

Groussac, Paul, 29

Guanahacabibes labor camp, 16–17

Guardia, Luis, 12

Guerilla Warfare (Guevara), 21–22

Guerra, Eutimio, 11

guerrilla warfare, Guevara's place in history of, 20–22

Guevara, Che
    on atomic war, 18
    as capitalist brand, 7–10
    Che Guevara cult members, 1–2, 8–9, 9–10
    discovery of remains, 8
    financial destruction of Cuba, 19–20
    and guerrilla warfare, 20–22
    photo ops for, 16
    violence of, 10–14

Guevara, Che, personal testimony of
    about, 10
    on Arbenz's failure to execute potential enemies, 11

Guevara, Che, personal testimony of
(*cont.*)
  on Bolivian peasants, 21
  on instructing "struggling masses" to
    rob banks, 15
  on Valdivia's craving for limitless
    power, 15
Guzmán, Abimael, 2

Harrison, Lawrence, 45
Hart, Keith, 65–66
Haya de la Torre, Victor Raúl, 29
Henry, Thierry, 9
Huerta de Soto, Jesús, 27–28
human relations, Latin America view
  of, 46–47
human rights as right to violate all
  rights, 41–42
hyperinflation, 30–31, 32

Iberian colonial system, 4, 26–28, 53
Improper Conduct (Almendros), 17
Incas, 54, 55–57, 67n2
independence movement, 61–64
Indian communities, free market in, 57
individual and individualism
  independence movement, 61–64
  individual-based rights, 5, 53–54
  informal economy as evidence of,
    66–67
  pre-Incan Empire private property
    rights, 56–57
  rule of law as will of society, not
    individuals, 41
industrialization of Cuba, 20
Infante, Tita, 11
informal economy, 39, 46, 54, 64–67
instability and/or stability issues in
  Latin America, 23–24
institutional organization, 24
institutions and culture (or culture and
  institutions), 44–48

intellectuals, poor morals and mediocre
  souls of, 49
interest groups and privileges, 34, 36–39
interventionism, 38

Jefferson, Thomas, 4
Jouvenel, Bertrand de, 24
Juárez, Benito, 29
justice
  citizens's mistrust of, 41
  corruption in, 40–41
  Guevara's homicidal idea of, 10
  as necessary for economic success, 36
  perception of state as agent of social
    justice, 4–5, 29–30
  productive system with, 3
  See also rule of law
Justinian, 41

Kabila, Laurent, 21
Khrushchev, 18
Kizner, Israel, 35
Korda, Alberto, 7
Kudriavtsev, Sergie, 16
kurakas of Inca Empire, 56, 57

La Cabaña prison, 12–14
labor camps in Cuba, 16–17
Lago, Armando, 14
land reform, 20
Las Siete Partidas, 58
Latin America
  colonization through 1990s, 26–30
  distrust of United States, 29, 48
  history of, 4, 22
  instability and/or stability issues,
    23–24
  origin of term, 67n1
  perception of state as agent of social
    justice, 4–5, 29–30
  reforms with mixed results, 30–33
  See also economics of Latin America;

politics of Latin America
Lavandeira, Alberto, 16
law. *See* rule of law
Lebanese demonstrators, 9
Leoni, Bruno, 40–41
Leung Kwok-hung, 9
liberal caudillos, 29
liberalism in republican times, 61–64
liberation of the mind, 3
Lima, Ariel, 13

Maoist China, 19
Maradona, 9
Mariana, Juan de, 28, 60
Mariátegui, José Carlos, 29
market economy
    in Argentina in 1830s to 1930s, 63
    of black market, 39, 46, 54, 64–67
    corrupt justice system preventing,
        40–41
    dictatorship as block to developing,
        43
    effect of privatization controlled by
        government, 35–36
    of Indian communities, 57
    and regulations and culture, 45
    separation of rule of law and, 25
    subjective nature of value, 60
    See also capitalism; economics of
        Latin America
Masetti, Jorge Ricardo, 20
Mayan culture, 54–55
Meiji Revolution (Japan), 45
Menem, Carlos, 35
Menoyo, Gutiérrez, 20
Mercado, Tomás de, 60
mercantilist marketplace, 40, 44, 56
"Message to the Tricontinental"
    (Guevara), 10
Mexica tribe, 55, 67n2
Mexican Revolution, 29
Mexico, commercial tradition in, 55

Mikoyan, Anastas, 18
Military Units to Help Production, 17
Minà, Gianni, 7
Miranda, Francisco de, 29, 36, 61
Mobuto, 21
Molina, Luis de, 60
monopolies, state-protected, 37, 43–44
Montoya, José Luis, 9
Motorcycle Diaries, The (movie), 7–8, 8
Mulele, Pierre, 21

Naipaul, V.S., 21, 46
Nasser, Gamal Abdel, 15
National Bank of Cuba, 19–20
National Institute of Agrarian Reform,
    Department of Industry, 19, 20
Nebrija, Antonio de, 27
nomocracy, 24
North, Douglass C., 40, 44–45
North American colonies, 26–27

objectives over laws formula for
    government, 24
O'Hagan, Sean, 7
Oltuski, Enrique, 15
open society, transition versus creation,
    34–36
Oppenheimer, Franz, 3, 36
oppression, 3–4, 53
Ortega y Gasset, José, 24

parasitical oligarchies, 3
pensions, 31, 38–39
Peru, Shining Path in, 2
Physiocrats, 61
Pinochet, Augusto, 24
Pizarro, Gonzalo, 54, 58–59
Planiol, 40
politics of Latin America
    chaos (except in Argentina), 28–29
    as foundation of economic reform,
        34–36, 39–44

politics of Latin America (*cont.*)
  kurakas of Inca Empire, 56, 57
  liberalism in republican times, 61–64
  property rights and, 42
  prospects for improvements, 48–50
  rational constructions and Comtian
    positivism, 28
  rebellion and independence
    movements, 27–28
  social welfare versus capitalism,
    29–30
  Spanish colonization, 26–27
  spiritual versus material values, 29
  See also capitalism
Politics of Obedience, The (Boétie), 3
populism, 63–64
Prebisch, Raúl, 30
pre-Columbian states, 26, 53, 54–57
predatory systems, 3
privatization
  with government control, 34–36, 37,
    39–40
  of land, by Peruvian farmers, 42
  moving toward, 31
  of politics, 48
productive system with justice, 3
property rights
  human rights and, 42
  pre-Incan, 56–57

Rangel, Carlos, 29, 67
rational constructionism, 28
rationality, liberal versus constructivist,
  28
rebellion, Pizarro's, 58–59
Reisman, George, 34
religion, Spanish control of, 27
Representación de Huamanga (Pizarro),
  59
revolution as license to reallocate
  property, 15
D'Rivera, Paquito, 14

Rodó, José Enrique, 29
Rodríguez, Félix, 14
Roman Catholic Church, 27
Rosario, Argentina, 8
Rosas, Juan Manuel, 22, 62
Rothbard, Murray, 42, 44
rule of law
  constitutional changes and, 25–26
  culture as insufficient without, 45–46
  democracy as different from, 41
  effect of dictatorship versus, 43
  informal economy as indication of
    possibility for, 66–67
  objectives over, 24
  separation of market economy and, 25
  as will of society, not individuals, 41
Ruskin gothic vision, 26–27
Russia, 17–19, 20

Salamancan scholars, 27–28, 54, 59–61
San Carlos de La Cabaña "La Cabaña
  prison," 12–14
Sancti Spiritus, Cuba, 15
Santa Clara, Cuba, 12, 20
Santana, Carlos, 10, 14
Saravia de la Calle, Luis, 28, 60
School of Salamanca, 27–28, 54, 59–61
Schumpeter, Joseph A., 29
Shining Path, 2
Sierra Maestra, 11
simultaneity of reforms, need for, 34–35
smuggling in seventeenth century, 27
socialism mixed with foreign
  investments, 30–33
Soto, Domingo de, 60
Soviet-Cuban negotiations, 18
sovietization of the revolution, 17–18
Spanish colonization of Latin America,
  4, 26–28, 53, 58–61
Spanish economists and humanists,
  27–28
spiritual values, development of, 29

stability and/or instability issues in Latin America, 23–24

statist position as root of underdevelopment, 4–5, 29–30, 53

Stavropol, Russia, 9

subsidies, 34, 35, 38, 42

"survival" (black) economy, 39, 46, 54, 64–67

Sydney, Australia, 9

Tarará, Cuba, 15–16

tariffs, 37–38

Telefónica, 37

teleocracy, 24

telephone systems, privatization of, 37

Telmex, 37

Tenochtitlán, 55

theoretical republics, 62

Thomas, Robert Paul, 40

Thomas Aquinas, Saint, 59

Tiahuanaco culture, 55, 56

Time (magazine), 17

Tlatelolco, 55

totalitarian tyrants
commonalities among, 2, 3–4
Guevara's admiration for, 15

trade, liberalization with privileges for wealthy, 37–38, 49

trade and property in ancient times, 54–57

transition from socialism to free society, 34–36

unemployment, 33, 35

Unidades Militares de Ayuda a la Producción, 17

United Nations, Guevara at, 18

Urquiza, Justo José de, 22

Uruguay, 29

Uruguay conference (1961), 19

U.S.-backed Bay of Pigs invasion, 16

Valdés, Ramiro, 12, 16

Valdivia, Pedro de, 15

Vallegrande airport, Bolivia, 8

value, discovery of subjective nature of, 60

Varela, José Pedro, 29

Vázquez, Jaime Costa, 12

Véliz, Claudio, 26–27

Venezuela, 38

Vera, Oscar, 42

Vilasuso, José, 12–13, 14

violence of Che Guevara, 10–14

Vitoria, Francisco de, 28, 60

Weyler, Valeriano, 16

Yucatán Peninsula, 54

Yupanqui, Túpac, 56

Yuro ravine, Guevara's capture at, 21

Acknowledgments

"The Killing Machine: Che Guevara, from Communist Firebrand to Capitalist Brand" originally appeared in *The New Republic* (July 11, 2005). Reprinted with permission.

"Latin American Liberalism—A Mirage?" originally appeared in the Winter 2002 issue of *The Independent Review* (Vol. 6, No. 3).

"The Individualist Legacy in Latin America" originally appeared in the Winter 2004 issue of *The Independent Review* (Vol. 8, No. 3).

About the Author

Alvaro Vargas Llosa is Senior Fellow and Director of the Center on Global Prosperity at the Independent Institute. A native of Peru, he received his B.S.C. in international history from the London School of Economics. He has been op-ed page editor at the *Miami Herald* and contributor to the *Wall Street Journal, New York Times, New Republic, Los Angeles Times, International Herald Tribune*, BBC, and *Time*. In addition, Mr. Vargas Llosa has been a commentator at Univision TV, Panamericana TV, and Radio Nacional de Espana; news director at RCN radio; correspondent for ABC; international affairs editor at *Expreso*; arts editor at *Oiga*; host of the weekly TV program "Planeta 3" (aired in twelve countries); and columnist at *La Nación, El Nacional, Reforma, El Tiempo, El País*, and *El Listín Diario*.

His books include *Liberty for Latin America*; *El Exilio Indomable*; *Cuando Hablaba Dormido*; *El Diablo en Campaña*; *En el Reino del Espanto*; *Tiempos de Resistencia*; *La Mestiza de Pizarro*; *La Contenta Barbarie*; *The Madness of Things Peruvian*; and *Guide to the Perfect Latin American Idiot* and *The Manufacturing of Poverty* (both with C. A. Montaner and P. A. Mendoza). And, Mr. Vargas Llosa is recipient of the A.I.R. Award for Best Current Affairs Radio Show in Florida, Puerto Rican Parliament Award for the Defense of Freedom, Award for the Defense of Freedom from the Peruvian Asociación de Pescadores Artesanales de Chimbote, and Freedom of Expression Award from the Association of Ibero-American Journalists.

INDEPENDENT STUDIES IN POLITICAL ECONOMY

THE ACADEMY IN CRISIS: The Political Economy of Higher Education | *Ed. by John W. Sommer*

AGAINST LEVIATHAN: Government Power and a Free Society | *Robert Higgs*

AGRICULTURE AND THE STATE: Market Processes and Bureaucracy | *E. C. Pasour, Jr.*

ALIENATION AND THE SOVIET ECONOMY: The Collapse of the Socialist Era | *Paul Craig Roberts*

AMERICAN HEALTH CARE: Government, Market Processes and the Public Interest | *Ed. by Roger D. Feldman*

ANTITRUST AND MONOPOLY: Anatomy of a Policy Failure | *D. T. Armentano*

ARMS, POLITICS, AND THE ECONOMY: Historical and Contemporary Perspectives | *Ed. by Robert Higgs*

BEYOND POLITICS: Markets, Welfare and the Failure of Bureaucracy | *William C. Mitchell & Randy T. Simmons*

THE CAPITALIST REVOLUTION IN LATIN AMERICA | *Paul Craig Roberts & Karen LaFollette Araujo*

CHANGING THE GUARD: Private Prisons and the Control of Crime | *Ed. by Alexander Tabarrok*

CUTTING GREEN TAPE: Toxic Pollutants, Environmental Regulation and the Law | *Ed. by Richard Stroup & Roger E. Meiners*

THE DIVERSITY MYTH: Multiculturalism and Political Intolerance on Campus | *David O. Sacks & Peter A. Thiel*

DRUG WAR CRIMES: The Consequences of Prohibition | *Jeffrey A. Miron*

THE EMPIRE HAS NO CLOTHES: U.S. Foreign Policy Exposed | *Ivan Eland*

ENTREPRENEURIAL ECONOMICS: Bright Ideas from the Dismal Science | *Ed. by Alexander Tabarrok*

FAULTY TOWERS: Tenure and the Structure of Higher Education | *Ryan C. Amacher & Roger E. Meiners*

FREEDOM, FEMINISM, AND THE STATE: An Overview of Individualist Feminism | *Ed. by Wendy McElroy*

HAZARDOUS TO OUR HEALTH?: FDA Regulation of Health Care Products | *Ed. by Robert Higgs*

HOT TALK, COLD SCIENCE: Global Warming's Unfinished Debate | *S. Fred Singer*

LIBERTY FOR WOMEN: Freedom and Feminism in the Twenty-First Century | *Ed. by Wendy McElroy*

MARKET FAILURE OR SUCCESS: The New Debate | *Ed. by Tyler Cowen & Eric Crampton*

MONEY AND THE NATION STATE: The Financial Revolution, Government and the World Monetary System | *Ed. by Kevin Dowd & Richard H. Timberlake, Jr.*

OUT OF WORK: Unemployment and Government in Twentieth-Century America | *Richard K. Vedder & Lowell E. Gallaway*

PLOWSHARES AND PORK BARRELS: The Political Economy of Agriculture | *E. C. Pasour, Jr. & Randal R. Rucker*

A POVERTY OF REASON: Sustainable Development and Economic Growth | *Wilfred Beckerman*

PRIVATE RIGHTS & PUBLIC ILLUSIONS | *Tibor R. Machan*

RECLAIMING THE AMERICAN REVOLUTION: The Kentucky & Virginia Resolutions and Their Legacy | *William J. Watkins, Jr.*

REGULATION AND THE REAGAN ERA: Politics, Bureaucracy and the Public Interest | *Ed. by Roger Meiners & Bruce Yandle*

RESTORING FREE SPEECH AND LIBERTY ON CAMPUS | *Donald A. Downs*

RESURGENCE OF THE WARFARE STATE: The Crisis Since 9/11 | *Robert Higgs*

RE-THINKING GREEN: Alternatives to Environmental Bureaucracy | *Ed. by Robert Higgs & Carl P. Close*

SCHOOL CHOICES: True and False | *John D. Merrifield*

STRANGE BREW: Alcohol and Government Monopoly | *Douglas Glen Whitman*

TAXING CHOICE: The Predatory Politics of Fiscal Discrimination | *Ed. by William F. Shughart, II*

TAXING ENERGY: Oil Severance Taxation and the Economy | *Robert Deacon, Stephen DeCanio, H. E. Frech, III, & M. Bruce Johnson*

THAT EVERY MAN BE ARMED: The Evolution of a Constitutional Right | *Stephen P. Halbrook*

TO SERVE AND PROTECT: Privatization and Community in Criminal Justice | *Bruce L. Benson*

THE VOLUNTARY CITY: Choice, Community and Civil Society | *Ed. by David T. Beito, Peter Gordon & Alexander Tabarrok*

WINNERS, LOSERS & MICROSOFT: Competition and Antitrust in High Technology | *Stan J. Liebowitz & Stephen E. Margolis*

WRITING OFF IDEAS: Taxation, Foundations, & Philanthropy in America | *Randall G. Holcombe*

For further information and a catalog of publications, please contact:

THE INDEPENDENT INSTITUTE

100 Swan Way, Oakland, California 94621-1428, U.S.A.

510-632-1366 · Fax 510-568-6040 · info@independent.org · www.independent.org